HOPE SPRINGS
FROM A MOTHER'S BROKEN HEART

HOPE SPRINGS FROM A MOTHER'S Broken Heart

11 Mothers Share
How They Survived
the Loss of a Child

BY
THERESA ANTHONY

ISBN: 978-0-578-92938-5

Library of Congress Control Number: 2021911645

Cover Design by Emma Anthony

Printed in the United States of America

First printing edition 2021

www.TheresaAnthony.com

This book is lovingly dedicated

to my mother, Sheila,

who lost her youngest daughter to cancer at age twenty-six,

and to all heartbroken mothers

who grieve the loss of a child

Contents

The Lord is close to the brokenhearted,

and saves those whose spirit is crushed.

PSALM 34:19 NAB

Introduction

On a crisp autumn day in 2013, my whole world fell apart. It was on October 23, 2013, that I lost my beautiful son to suicide. Just typing those words still sends chills up my spine. The shock of losing him that day will forever remain a jagged scar permanently etched on my heart.

My handsome, kind-hearted son began struggling with mental health issues during his first year of college. This led to alcohol abuse, and eventually alcoholism. After a heroic effort during his last year of life to overcome the disease of alcoholism, he could fight no more.

After Matthew's death, I became one of the walking wounded, a member of a club that no one would ever want to belong to. I was a grieving mother. I made my way through each day in a zombie-like, half-dead daze. I struggled to even know what day it was, much less the season, and could barely manage even the most mundane daily tasks. Although I felt mortally wounded by the loss of my son, it was worse than that, being instead the kind of wound that maims you but doesn't take you out.

In the weeks and months following his death, friends and acquaintances kindly guided me toward other women who had also lost a child. It was suggested that I join a local Facebook group called

Grieving Mommas, a support group started by Gina, a woman you will read about later. Gina had lost her sweet ten-year-old boy to a rare disease several years earlier. Through her Facebook group, I was invited to a dinner where I would meet several of the women from the group in person. And I was astounded.

These women were lovely, poised, grace-filled people—nothing like the haggard mess I was back in those early days. Each mom had lost their child to various causes, but there we were, bound together by our common identity as women who had suffered the worst experience imaginable. I remember thinking that evening, "Wow, I could only *hope* to someday function as well as they do." At that early juncture in my grief journey, the chances of that seemed very, very remote.

At about that same time, one of the moms from the group, Kathy, who had also lost a son to suicide, reached out to invite me to an event at Saddleback Church, the mega-church headed by Pastor Rick Warren. It was hosting its first ever Survivors of Suicide Loss Day and she thought I might benefit from going. Even though it had been mere weeks since my son's death, I summoned the strength to attend this important event with her.

After the initial gathering in the hall, we were instructed to break out into groups based on the role the deceased person had in our life. I headed to the room sadly labeled, "Child." I entered the room to find a group of about twenty people seated around a long conference-style table, and took a seat. I was really surprised that this many parents had also lost a son or daughter to suicide. One at a time, the attendees introduced themselves and shared the name of their child and the year they had lost them. Eventually, it was time for the woman seated next to me to take her turn. She introduced herself as Kay Warren. I immediately realized this was Rick Warren's wife. The Warrens had lost their son, Matthew, who suffered from debilitating depression, just that April. This event had been organized by her to provide much needed support for suicide loss survivors.

Kay Warren is what most would describe as a tower of strength. She left a deep impression on me that day. I was full of admiration for this grieving mother. She had summoned the strength, just months after her son's death, to honor his memory by creating a source of support for others. Her Survivors of Suicide Loss events have continued at Saddleback Church every year since. I have since learned that she founded the Hope for Mental Health Community, a forum for those who struggle, or have a loved one who struggles, with mental health disorders, and she also organizes the BREATHE Retreats for parents.

That day, during the mid-morning break between sessions, I wandered out to the lobby area to grab a beverage. As I walked through the corridor, I came upon a vendor booth where a woman, Kathryn, had set up a large assortment of suicide loss support materials, leaflets and such, for people who had lost a loved one. Her business was named after the son she'd lost: Lil' Gary's Legacy. I browsed through the various materials, as well as her family scrapbooks where I read about her son. I remember being so impressed. Somehow, this mother had found the strength to write and publish all these materials to help other parents who, sadly, found themselves in the same boat.

This day at Saddleback Church was only the very beginning of my trek into this new world. One person introduced me to another, and soon I was attending community events held at a local church. There I met several women who had also lost young adult children, primarily to drug overdoses. I sat there with a lump in my throat listening to these mothers passionately describe the child they'd lost and their missions to warn and inform teens, young adults, and parents about the dangers of these substances.

One mother who got up and spoke, Jodi Barber, really stood out. She had produced two documentaries that she widely distributes to schools across the country. These compelling videos, targeting middle and high school-age students, present the cold, hard facts about the dangers of drugs. As she stood in front of the audience, I noticed her calm, measured delivery of the important message she was sharing with the parents in the community who had taken the time to attend. I was in awe, wondering how she didn't burst into tears when sharing about the prescription opioids that had taken her beautiful nineteen-year-old son, Jarrod's, life. In my depleted state at that time, I couldn't imagine ever being so purposeful and passionate. She really impressed me, and will also impress you when you read her story in the upcoming pages.

People who grieve the loss of a loved one are familiar with that old adage, "time heals all wounds," even if it isn't necessarily true. However, now that seven years have passed, I can say that the passage of time does give you a chance to reboot your broken spirit. After enough time has passed, your spirit does eventually re-emerge. In time, although battered and bruised on the inside and a tad more haggard on the outside, I experienced the resurrection of my spirit, eventually discovering my own unique way to honor my son's memory.

At the time of my son's death, I had been a freelance writer for about fifteen years. Not even a year had passed when I knew what I would do; I would try to help people by directing my writing skills toward the behavioral health field. Just eight months after losing Matthew, I took a position as a content writer specializing in the fields of mental health and addiction recovery. My mission was to use my writing abilities to hopefully inspire people to seek help, and to do so before it is too late.

Then, in 2019, I took this newly defined purpose to the next level and wrote a memoir entitled *My 13th Station: A Mother Shares Her*

Son's Tragic Battle with Depression, Alcoholism, and Demons. Since its publication, I have received countless messages from mothers and fathers who reached out to thank me for writing a book that had deeply touched them, one they could, unfortunately, very much relate to. Receiving these messages always brings tears to my eyes and fills me with the most wonderful sense of accomplishment. My son's story is helping others.

When 2020 was drawing to a close, I was feeling a bit rudderless, without any sense of direction for the upcoming turn of the calendar. While living through the pandemic, it became hard to focus on things like personal goals and dreams. Sheer survival had taken the top priority spot in most of our lives. So there I was, considering the New Year and lamenting that I just didn't know what I should do next.

And then, like a bolt of lightning, inspiration came to me. I decided then and there that it was time to write a second book. I would write a useful and empowering guidebook for mothers who have lost a son or daughter. I would share my own insights about the grieving process, things I have learned from my personal experience these past seven years, but I would also showcase some of the strong, purpose-filled women I have come to know. I didn't want the book to focus only on the pain and heartache of losing a child; I wanted to inspire hope.

I was thrilled to have ten mothers agree to join me in sharing their own soulful, courageous stories. I am abundantly honored that they were willing to open their hearts and allow us a glimpse inside. These women are impressive and strong, heroic examples of grace in action.

When envisioning this book, I saw each mother painting her own unique portrait of resilience in the wake of tragic loss. Because each contributing mother has her own unique voice, personality, and perspective, and with a variety of causes of death among the children,

I am convinced that any grieving mother reading this book will be able to personally connect with at least one of them.

In the upcoming pages you will learn a bit about each of us, about our children, and about the diverse ways we have managed to navigate our own grief journeys. You will learn about the tools we have relied upon to get us through the bleak days. The mothers share a wide range of coping tools, things like family support, faith, music, grief therapy, setting fitness goals, creative pursuits, and the spearheading of projects. This book, therefore, becomes an important and relevant source of strength for a newly grieving mother to draw upon—grief *support*, versus a collection of platitudes.

For any mother who has found herself in this sad club, it is my sincere hope that you take away from this book a sense of validation about your own grief experience, as well as a newfound freedom to work through it at your own pace and in your own way. There is no single "best way" to navigate the hidden landmines that you will encounter along the grief journey. But in reading about how the eleven of us have managed to survive, this book will hopefully become a welcome source of encouragement.

Most of all, I pray these personal stories of loss and restoration leave you feeling inspired. Yes, life without your child probably lacks the sparkle it once had, but it still, nevertheless, manages to go on. Indeed, like a survival instinct buried deep within a mother's DNA, there is an innate need to preserve ourselves. And so, as unlikely as it may seem, a mother's broken heart really *does* provide fertile ground for a surprising resurgence of hope.

PART ONE

Mothers Living With a Hole in Their Hearts

CHAPTER 1

A Day in the Life of a Grieving Mother

There it is, like a morning kiss peeking above the hilltops to greet me each day when I emerge from my bedroom . . . the sun. That brilliant ray of sunshine is my morning reminder that I have survived yet another day. How many days have I awakened, still groggy in the post-dream state and not yet cognizant of what is missing from my life? It takes a few seconds for my brain to connect with my heart, and then it clicks; that unwelcome communiqué: my son is gone.

Mind you, the loss of my son, Matthew, is not a fresh one. It has been over seven years since that dark day when I said my last goodbye to him in the emergency room at our local hospital. And therein lies the mystery. How is it that, regardless of how many days, weeks, months, or years have passed, the pain of losing him remains stubbornly alive in every fiber of my being?

As I write this, it has been 2,645 days since Matthew died. Each and every day has been a contest, a battle waged inside my heart to determine whether I will emerge the next day victorious, or if I myself will die of this grief. I wake up each morning never knowing how each day will play out. Some days I skip along and hit the sack feeling smug and in control, while other days I barely limp my way through the hours, wishing—begging—for heaven to take me by the time my tear-soaked face finally touches the pillow. Yes, to be sure there are some very rough days. Fortunately, as each day stacks on top of the last, the bad days have mercifully become fewer.

But alas, here I am, standing at the window greeting a brand-new morning. Before me spans a whole day to fill with meaningful and productive pursuits that will hopefully include many opportunities to glorify God in some way. I usually begin my days in a very positive state of mind. It isn't forced or fake; it is just my nature to be hopeful and positive. Who knows, though, where the day will go as it unfolds?

I have become quite comfortable in my daily routine, that series of activities that now serves to distract me from myself. Like many people, I plan the day's activities while mindlessly eating breakfast, sipping my morning tea, and catching the news updates. By maintaining these lifelong habits, I am able to feel somewhat normal, as if I am still a regular, functioning human.

Reality starts to set in, though, after my shower. While engaging in the routine hair drying and beautification rituals, there is no avoiding my reflection in the mirror. This is the time each morning when I am confronted with my truth, revealed in the sad eyes looking back at me in the mirror. You can see it, you know, the pain. No matter what measures I take to present myself to the world each day, or how many times I smile or chuckle while chatting with a friend, my eyes are the dead giveaway. Mine are the eyes of a grieving mother.

I recognize the same sorrow in the eyes of other grieving moms I have come to know over the past few years. We share the same eyes, just in varying hues. Some have sad brown eyes; some have sad blue eyes. But whatever the color, no matter how stunning, all of these eyes are bathed in sadness. I bet that mothers who have lost a child, no matter what the cause of death, can be picked out of a crowd simply by their sorrow-filled eyes.

As I apply my eye pencil, I wonder how many times I will think of Matt today. How often will I catch the tears in my throat? How many memories of him will be triggered by something I hear or see along the course of the day? How many times will I smile at his pictures, framed in the hallway, on my bookcase, in my bedroom? Sometimes I look at his picture and am astonished that this boy I gave birth to is now the subject I write about—about losing him, grieving him, and how desperately I long to hug him. In my mind and heart, I still feel like I am mothering him, communicating with him from earth to heaven by some secret telecommunication system. I put the eye makeup away and sigh. Even all these years later, I still have to push myself through many heavy thoughts and emotions each and every day.

So, on I go about my day, dragging that broken heart around with me. I go to great lengths to hide the oozing sight from others, careful not to impose my own heartache on loved ones, colleagues, or the guy ringing up the groceries. I smile; I chat; I transact. I am adept at hiding behind my public visage. But just beneath the surface, they lurk, the tears just dying to flow, to gush, to release all the pent-up sorrow. Sometimes it is all I can do to keep up that brave front until I get home and can let it all out.

The bulk of my days involve scurrying from project to project. Of course, I realize that keeping busy is a coping tool. By focusing my attention on whatever populates the day's to-do list, I am protected from actually feeling the ache in my heart. So, I work hard at my job, I work out, I take daily walks and pray the rosary, I visit a friend or a daughter, I call my mom, and I work on my art. For me, staying busy and productive just works. Each grieving mom finds her own unique methods for safely navigating her days.

The waning hours of the day, after my work is done and I begin winding down, can be a vulnerable time. Because it is quiet, it's the perfect time for thoughts and memories to bubble back up to the surface. Sometimes I just sit there and stare off into space, trance like, as if I am still in shock even after all this time has passed. It is in this stillness that I become acutely aware that I am different now; I am profoundly changed from the inside out.

In the evening I usually take a few minutes to reflect and pray. During this time, I conjure up the blessings of the day, acknowledging anything good or positive that happened during the long hours when I had no option but to be wide awake, coherent, and operational. Gratefully, there are still many beautiful moments to be had, filled by the smiles of a grandchild, the chuckles shared with a girlfriend, or the gorgeous glimpses of nature encountered on a hike. But even though I take note of my many blessings, it is during these quiet, reflective moments that I miss my son the most.

By the time I crawl into bed, I am ready to shut down my consciousness and take a break for seven or eight hours—to forget my reality. I sink into the darkness and welcome any forthcoming dreams. Feeling a small sense of accomplishment, I drift off to sleep. Yes, I survived. I made it through another day without my boy.

CHAPTER 2

The Hidden Reservoir of Strength

I don't like being the one to tell a newly grieving mother about the struggles that lie ahead. I would love to paint a pretty picture of the grief journey, to assure them that "time heals." But those kinds of broad-stroke platitudes often defy reality. The truth is that each mother is wired in her own unique way to process emotional pain, trauma, and loss. The grief journey is nuanced and mysterious, ebbing and flowing over wild rapids some days and floating smoothly downriver on others. The one constant that defines a mother's grief experience, a common denominator that all grieving moms can undoubtedly agree upon, is that of being left with a broken heart.

But even with all that pain hiding away in our fractured little hearts, people seem to be rather amazed at our survival skills. I, too, am surprised by this innate ability to forge ahead. Some attribute it to a grace, a blessing, the fruits of a strong faith. Others say it is born of necessity, that the harsh and unrelenting demands of daily life do not cut a grieving mother any special slack. After all, we still need to function, pay our bills, and continue being there for our surviving children, spouse, family, and friends. I say it's a little of each.

Finding ways to manage the pain while working around the loss and resulting grief can help each one of us live as full a life as possible. It's about moving ahead each morning *after* confronting our sad eyes in the bathroom mirror. Our days begin at that pivotal moment of reckoning, of facing our truth in the reflection, which acts as a kind of launching pad. From there, we face the coming hours with the hope of offering some goodness to the world, of finding some purpose to help propel us through the day.

It might be hard to believe that a grieving mother is a woman who possesses a particular kind of strength, a superhuman strength, really. Think about it. We are able to go about our days, even while fully aware that our child has passed away. We don't cower in the closet or hide under the blankets. We function. A mysterious and beautiful ability, one that can only come from God, allows us to continue to be productive, inspiring, creative, and compassionate members of society. This is the mystery, the thing that we moms could have never imagined on that fateful day—that we could still be able to squeeze something meaningful out of our remaining days. It is this most uncanny and uniquely feminine strength that I hope to spotlight.

If you have lost a child, or know someone dear to you who has, you may already be aware of the intense nature of grief. If you have lost a child, maybe you sat inside your own dark closet in the wee hours howling like an animal, as I did. Or maybe you felt tortured in witnessing that kind of visceral pain emanating from a loved one when their child passed away. In those early hours, weeks, and months after the loss, it is next to impossible to imagine the restoration of spirit that does eventually occur. Indeed, back in that initial raw agony, survival itself seems iffy. Many of us will attest to going to bed each night wishing we'd never wake up again. That's how painful it is to lose a child.

But the human spirit is complex, resourceful, and powerful. Like a diver emerging from the deep, our spirits bubble back up to the surface to draw in just enough air to survive. Although hidden under layers of sorrow for a time, an innate resilience is embedded deep inside that spirit. Our human spirit is not done with us yet; it kicks and punches its way back into view. In fact, when you first notice the faint flicker of life still burning inside you, it may come as a shock. You may have assumed that, as a grief-stricken mother, you were destined to remain like the living dead in perpetuity. Not so fast.

For me, I realized my soul wasn't dead yet when I found myself dancing in the kitchen one day—shocking because I hadn't even given myself permission to dance, or to feel any joy whatsoever at that two-year mark. I remember even feeling guilty, as if I didn't deserve the moment of joy that spurred my feet to start moving like that. But just wait and see; your moment will come, too. And when your human spirit does show up again, embrace it. Know that any new signs of life, any joy you experience, is simply a testament to God's amazing grace. He has gifted you with resilience and armed you with some pretty special feminine superpowers. God wants you to laugh again. He wants you to sing and dance and experience joy, so try to allow Him to rebuild your spirit.

You might know someone else in your life who has survived the loss of a child. If you do, you probably learned a lot from them, things you can draw upon in your own grief. In my case, I witnessed my own mother get her feet back under her after the death of my sister, her youngest child, in 1985. As my little sister lay dying of breast cancer at the age of twenty-six, my mother held one of her hands while I held the other. Selfishly, at the time I viewed the loss of my sister through my own me-centered prism of pain, not really stopping to consider how badly it must have hurt my mom. So bereaved was I with the loss of my sister that I couldn't even fathom the depths of my mother's pain.

After some time had passed, it dawned on me how surprisingly strong my mother was. She never struck me as the strong, stoic type, but the way she managed her daily life as she moved forward displayed immense courage and strength. She returned to her job as a kindergarten teacher, barely missing a beat. She managed to keep her emotions in check, publicly anyway, something that I was clearly unable to do after my sister's death. My mother's generation is less open about expressing their personal hardships and tends to suffer in silence. My mom continued to teach for a couple more years before retiring at age fifty-five, and then began a new career as a travel agent.

I could have never known then, back in the late eighties, that the grace with which my mother handled herself after the death of her young daughter would serve as a role model for me. For it was in 1988, just three years after we lost my sister, that my son was born, only to be lost twenty-five years later. I know now, in living through the devastating reality of my own grieving mother story, that I sorely underestimated my mother's inner strength. Even now, at age eighty-eight, my mother laughs and smiles and enjoys life. I can see now that I gather much of my own ability to remain engaged and hopeful in life, even after a terrible loss, from having been my mother's daughter.

TREAD TENDERLY

You are about to enter the very hearts and souls of eleven courageous mothers who were willing to share their very personal accounts of grief following the loss of their child. Each one of the ten mothers who join me struggled immensely while writing their chapters, experiencing intense pain and shedding many tears.

To be able to convey the emotions and details of the loss of their precious son or daughter required these brave mothers to dig deep, unearthing the memories that had left such painful wounds. But each grieving mother you'll encounter in the coming pages sincerely hopes to offer some modicum of solace and hope for the person who now holds these pages in her hands.

I recommend you digest one mother's story at a sitting, as each of their stories is so very moving and rich. My hope and prayer is that you end each chapter feeling a sense of admiration, connection, and fellowship.

SPECIAL THANKS TO THESE MOTHERS

Gina Cousineau
Jodi Barber
Carmen Lofgren
Sharon "Sam" Randlett Major
Maggie Fleitman
Sandy Barker
Karon Hurlbut
Suzanne Williams
Elizabeth Moersch
Janice E.

CHAPTER 3

My Story

My name is Theresa Anthony, and I am just a regular, run-of-the-mill, sixty-something female residing in California. As a native Californian, I have lived in this beautiful state most of my life, with the exception of a few years during my early childhood. I am the mother to three beautiful children, two of whom reside on this planet, and one who now lives in heaven.

I have a bachelor's degree in human services (yes, back in the seventies social sciences were all the rage) and work as a freelance writer and author. Although I have experienced some career successes, what I am most proud of are the ten years I spent as a stay-at-home mom. As a child I had moved eight times by the time I entered high school, so my wish as a mother was to provide a stable, normal childhood for my children.

The irony is that I have always had a "Type A," very driven personality, always planning for my bright future and dreaming big dreams. I was a big list maker. I had one-year goals, five-year goals, and ten-year goals. I aspired to be a successful business owner and never doubted in my abilities to achieve that goal. What I didn't factor into all those lofty plans was life itself.

Sometimes in our quest to seek a dream or reach a goal, we ignore God's plan for our life and attempt to muscle our way against His current. For me, I had to experience the closure of my stores, and all the disappointment and loss that went with that, before finding myself drawn toward a totally different direction for my life. There I was in 1998, after my business closed, a mother of three children aged twelve, ten, and six, suddenly and strangely drawn to the simplicity of living a domestic life. This was quite the shock to me, as I had always planned on working outside the home, at least part-time. But in 1998, with a pile of books on homeschooling on my nightstand, I was excited to enter this mysterious new career as a stay-at-home/homeschool mom.

Although my marriage was extremely difficult and painful, I nevertheless endured, determined never to break up my beautiful family. For me, divorce simply was not an option. At the age of forty-two, I returned to my Catholic roots and became very devoted to the faith. I truly spent years praying for my marriage, but unfortunately it was doomed to fail. So, in late 2005, I became a divorced mother of three. And it was hard, very hard.

At this point in time, my children were nineteen, seventeen, and thirteen. I am forever grateful for my wonderful kids. They were, each one, well adjusted, kind, and thoughtful young humans. I had no problems with any of them, zero. My oldest daughter, Sarah, was about to start college; my son, Matthew, was a junior at the local high school; and my youngest, Emma, was still homeschooling at the time of the divorce.

It took time for us to adjust to being a broken family, but we carried on. I started back out in the workforce from scratch, earning a small salary and struggling to make ends meet. My kids were my top priority, so I did whatever it took to continue guiding them toward their own next steps in life. Together our little fractured family moved forward. In late 2006, Sarah, now age twenty, was doing well at college; Matt, eighteen, had graduated from high school and had set off to Cal Poly San Luis Obispo to study engineering; and Emma, fourteen, was about to start high school at a local Catholic school.

It was at this time that something changed in Matt. Formerly, for the entire first 18½ years of his life, he had been a happy, positive guy.

As a child he was any parent's delight, very kind, loving, and responsible. I nicknamed him Boy Blue, which in later years was truncated to just "Blue." He excelled at baseball, was tall and handsome, was a good student, and had really great friends. The years raising Matt were utterly delightful in every way. He was as solid as the day is long.

So, when he began to complain about chronic insomnia during his first semester at college, I just figured he was having difficulty adjusting to the college environment. By the fall of 2006, Matt was clearly struggling with depression. He was not at all himself. Surrounded by young adults at college, he began to party with them. At first he was trying to self-medicate the insomnia with alcohol and weed. As the months went on, however, he began to increasingly lean on the alcohol to manage the terrible depression that had set in.

As his mother, it was excruciating to watch him suffer. I did the mom things, having him see the doctor and get blood work done to see if there were any clues as to what was going on with him. I had him see a therapist, but after one session he refused to go back. At the end of the freshman year, he announced that he hated engineering and wanted to pursue his previous ambition since childhood, which was to become a firefighter. I supported this one hundred percent, just wanting him to be happy.

Sadly, his mental condition worsened over the next two years. He now suffered from depression, anxiety, and alcohol use disorder. His mental state became increasingly unstable. The alcohol problem just escalated like a runaway train, and by the age of twenty-one he was fully alcoholic. He had to leave the fire science program that year due to the fact that he and his girlfriend were expecting a baby. He needed a job to help support his family and the only job he could find at the depths of the Great Recession was a graveyard shift working in hotel security.

As his mother, I was beside myself. I was witnessing his life just crumbling before my eyes. As many a mom in this situation does, I became a co-dependent enabler. I was stomping out fires left and right, attempting to salvage his hoped-for career as a firefighter. First he was cited for underage drinking on the beach at age nineteen, and then cited again at age twenty when caught leaving a bar with a beer in his hand. Each offense was a mark against him, seriously threatening any hopes of ever being hired by a fire department.

And then there was all of the financial enabling. I paid his bills, paid his overdue traffic tickets; the list goes on. All I did by engaging in these "heroic" efforts was to keep him comfortable in his addiction. Why would he change if all his needs were being met?

Matt and Amanda married, and then, in March 2010, Amanda gave birth to a beautiful baby girl, Grace, my first grandchild. My hope was that with a wife and daughter, surely Matt would get his life together. Sadly, that was not the case. Working the graveyard shift only added to his loneliness and depression, and keeping that schedule was quite unhealthy for him.

I started to read books about addiction. I honestly had no past experience with this monster and needed to understand the foe that was trying to steal my child. Meanwhile, by 2012, Matt was sinking deeper into the disease, now chemically dependent on alcohol. His hands shook if he didn't drink. The facial bloating, glassy red eyes, and distended belly distorted his once handsome looks. Another attempt to get him into therapy failed, as he only attended three sessions before quitting yet again. I became worried sick. To make matters worse, his marriage broke up and he was absolutely devastated. Gracie was just two years old.

A glimmer of hope arrived in September of 2012 when Matt reached out and said he was ready for help, that he needed treatment or he felt he would die. This was an answer to many prayers! I volunteered to come to Colorado, where they had been living for eighteen months, to help out with Gracie while he was in rehab.

So, I took a leave of absence and for the next month I lived in his apartment in Vail while he was in treatment down the mountain in a Denver suburb. It was a truly beautiful month filled with the happy sounds of a 2½-year-old, a gorgeous mountain setting, and seeing my son slowly breaking the grip of the disease.

Three times a week I drove down the mountain to see Matt in rehab. I often joined the family therapy sessions, and sometimes I took Grace along to help keep him motivated and focused on the big prize, being with her again. She was truly all he lived for. He was such a devoted daddy, and just treasured his little girl.

When he was discharged from rehab after one month, I was so hopeful. Gracie and I drove down the hill so ecstatic to bring him home. We spent a few more days together, the three of us, and then it was time for me to let them reconnect as father and daughter. Matt located a local A.A. chapter and also set up an appointment for outpatient therapy. As hard as it was to leave them both, I drove back to

California totally (naively) convinced that he had licked this demon and that he was on his way to living a joy-filled life.

Sadly, it was less than a week before the bubble burst. I received a phone call from a sheriff informing me that Matt had jumped off the fourth floor of his apartment building and was being airlifted down to a level-one trauma center in Denver. To this day, eight years later, I can still feel the physical response I experienced upon hearing this news. I sank to the floor and could barely eek out a reply to the sheriff on the other end. He gave me the hospital contact information and I hung up the phone. Feeling sick to my stomach, I crawled to the doorway of my bedroom, trying to muster up enough sound to call out to my daughter, Emma, whose room was at the far end of the hall.

In that moment, twenty-year-old Emma became the mother. She hoisted me up from the floor to my bed. She brought me a glass of water and demanded that I take sips. She reminded me to breathe. She did all this while sobbing for her poor brother. Once my daughter Sarah was informed, she showed up at the house, just as devastated. She made me a smoothie while trying to console me. The reality was sinking in. Matt had relapsed and attempted suicide.

Matt's injuries were horrific. When he jumped, he slammed into a steel handrail and hit the concrete steps, which he had surely been aiming for. He had a huge gash on his scalp with twenty-five staples holding it together. He had six broken ribs, a broken clavicle, and the worst injuries of all were to his left leg. There was a very deep laceration from his buttock to his knee with a huge hematoma, and then what looked like a massive shark bite on his shin. At one point there was talk of amputation. My ex-husband and I were told it was nothing short of a miracle that this 215 pound, 6'3" man had survived that fall. I credited his guardian angel.

Although Matt eventually recovered from all the injuries, this incident marked the beginning of the end of his life. For the next year, he made a heroic effort to sustain sobriety so that he could start rebuilding his life with Gracie. He had lost everything—his job, his apartment, and his parental rights—due to the suicide attempt. He tried so hard, but his journey was uphill all the way.

In 2013, Matt moved back to California to be closer to all his family and some of his local friends, and stayed for a while in a sober living home while he got stronger. But every so many months, the wily foe that is alcoholism would reassert itself and he would relapse. Each time he relapsed, he was filled with shame, guilt, and despair.

A parallel aspect to Matt's suffering was the horrible spiritual warfare he had been afflicted with for the past several years. When you have the devil telling you that you are a worthless loser undeserving of love, it is very hard to battle off the mental health and addiction disorders. It is all interconnected.

That year, 2013, was a terrible year in my life. All the while my son was struggling with his problems, I was the primary caregiver for my love, Mike, who had been diagnosed with a deadly form of leukemia. The caregiving entailed trips to Stanford while he was in the process of being properly diagnosed with a rare form of leukemia called C.M.M.L., as well as multiple doctor visits, ongoing transfusions, and managing eighteen medications.

Meeting Mike in 2010 was a blessing that I will forever be grateful to God for having arranged. After being single for almost five years, I had given up hope of ever finding true love. Ah, but God knows stuff. He knew that at a given point in time I would need Mike, and that Mike would need me, although back in 2011 when we started dating, we had no inkling of these upcoming trials. To me, he was the knight in shining armor who rode in just as I had given up on love. He was a decent, kind, generous man. He was hard working and handsome. Mostly, Mike treasured me, and I him.

That summer of 2013, when he was so ill, I had him move in with me so I could care for him. In September, his leukemia took a deadly turn and he was hospitalized with the fatal A.M.L. We were told that Mike would need a stem cell transplant to have any chance of survival, and that he'd need to spend months tethered to the hospital.

He lost forty pounds over the next month as the chemo and the disease took their toll on him. In fact, the doctor discharged him on October 18th to come home for a couple of weeks so I could fatten him up prior to his stem cell transplant. There are no coincidences. God timed everything out perfectly.

Although Matt had relapsed back on Labor Day, he had been stable for seven weeks at this point. He was very engaged in his recovery efforts, going to A.A. meetings every morning at 7:00 am and working the Twelve Steps with a sponsor. He was looking for work, due to that last relapse having cost him his job. He had come so far since the horrible injuries sustained the prior year. In recovery, he looked really great, fit and tan. He ate healthy foods, worked out or hiked almost daily, and was socializing with his old baseball friends from high school again. Matt was in a good place, and looking forward to Gracie coming for a visit on the 29th of October.

On October 23rd, Mike and I were headed out early to spend several hours at the hospital to be prepped for the stem cell transplant. Matt had been staying with us the last couple of months while he got his life back in order. That morning he asked me if we still had tennis rackets, because he and a friend were going to hit balls. He told me that Sarah had asked him to babysit Jake, my two year-old grandson, from 4:00-8:00 pm. He was happy that Sarah even offered to pay him. We crossed paths in the hallway on our way out, as he was off to attend his 7:00 am meeting as usual. Mike turned to him and said, "Matt, you are doing a great job. Keep it up."

Tragically, my son took his life at about 10:15 am that morning.

I will have lifelong P.T.S.D. from this event because I don't believe the shock will ever wear off. No one, absolutely no one, saw it coming. By the time we were alerted to something being wrong, it was too late. The heroic efforts of the police and paramedics, for which I am forever grateful, were not provided in time to bring him back from the carbon monoxide poisoning.

When I arrived at the emergency room of the local hospital, I was certain Matt would be getting up and walking out of there. I couldn't accept that God would have allowed him to actually die. But when I entered the small bay where he lay lifeless, the priest I'd had my daughter call standing at the head of the bed, and my ex-husband in a chair sobbing, I just lost it. I came completely unglued.

I commanded Matt to wake up. I told him I was there to save him, to please open his eyes. The reality began to set in. My teeth were chattering and I began stomping my feet, shouting, "Wake up, Matthew, wake up!" The grief counselor assigned to our family offered me a chair, and into it I slumped. My beautiful Boy Blue was gone. I wrapped my fingers into his still warm hand and told him how much I loved him, and just how wonderful a son he was. And then I said goodbye.

Matt had left a handwritten letter to his daughter on his desk. When she is a grown adult I will make sure she receives this sweet, beautiful, heartbreaking letter. He wrote that he felt we were all better off without him. That he was a failure. The lies of the devil.

I will be forever grateful that God had arranged for the doctors to discharge Mike at that time, just before his transplant. I would not have made it through that horrible day, and the upcoming weeks, without his love and support. Eventually, Mike returned to the hospital for the stem cell transplant, and I became a fixture at his side. It was very difficult, spending eight to ten hours a day as Mike's main source of support while being so emotionally devastated after losing Blue. I was on fumes, but Mike needed me and I wouldn't let him down.

My grief journey was immensely compounded when, just nine months later, Mike succumbed to the leukemia. I honestly felt like I would not survive the pain. All the grieving mothers I have come to know personally have spouses or a significant other at their side. Enduring the loss of my precious son, and then my beautiful man, the love of my life, has been beyond difficult. Six months after Matt died, my dog had to be put down. A month after Mike died, my dad passed away. Those were a couple of really horrible years.

My daughters grieved the loss of their brother terribly. They soldiered on, Emma in an intensive program at Art Center College of Design, and Sarah in her roles as mother, wife, and teacher. They, too, didn't have the space they needed to grieve. Somehow, though, as a heartbroken family, we all muddled through.

I can't tell you how many times I hear, "How do you even get out of bed in the morning?" or "Wow, I can't believe how well you are doing!" Going through so much grief and loss in a compressed time frame is absolutely awful. I honestly lost about two years, not even aware of what month it was or which season we were in. I was shell-shocked, just barely functioning. On the outside, though, I still tried to project a positive attitude. I guess I was trying to avoid being seen as the pathetic lady whose son had taken his own life. I didn't want to be pitied. But for parents whose children die a stigmatized death, like a suicide or an overdose, pity does come with the territory. Not only pity, but discomfort and avoidance, too. It is too much for many people to process or comprehend.

Surviving the loss of a child, regardless of the cause of death, takes immense effort and strength. It also takes a lot of support, even if you don't know you need it. I was referred to a grief counselor who worked with me for about a year. That was tremendously helpful, just to have somewhere safe and nurturing to go where I could bawl my eyes out for an hour each week. She was kind and sensitive, and guided me through that first terrible year of loss.

As time went on, I decided that I still wanted to live after all, and began to focus more attention on self-care. I finally went grocery shopping and bought a whole cartful of food, something I had not done since Mike died. It was very strange loading up my shopping cart full of food, but I guess, looking back, it was a turning point.

In 2015, because I had become weak physically, I set some new fitness goals. I first joined a boot camp and then joined Orange Theory, which is a high-intensity interval training program. These programs helped whip me into shape. And then I discovered Zumba dance fitness. These fun dance cardio classes marked a pivotal point in my grief recovery. Although I was awkward and self-conscious trying to follow along at first, I eventually learned the steps. In addition to the fun dance choreography, I made some friends in the Zumba classes, too, and soon found myself smiling as I shimmied and shook my way across the floor to the Latin beats.

I also channeled my pain into making Catholic-themed crafts and jewelry, and started a new business venture on Etsy. This creative outlet helped fill the crushingly lonely evenings when all the sad emotions seemed to bubble up to the surface. In fact, I have found the whole crafting process extremely therapeutic. I play my favorite music and sing along as I create the lovely items that require me to focus for hours on images of Jesus, Mary, and the saints as I make them. To date, I have sold over three hundred pieces on Etsy, and another four hundred at craft shows and via word-of-mouth custom orders, which makes me really happy.

I returned to the corporate workplace, where I worked as a staff writer, a few weeks after Mike passed away. I quickly learned that I was unable to sit there at a desk and act normal for eight hours a day.

I was simply in too much pain. So I decided, at about the same time in 2015 that I started the Etsy business, to take a leap of faith and start my own freelance content writing business.

Six years later, I am happy to say that this venture has also been a success. I knew that, for me anyway, surviving the losses meant staying productive and forward focused. I had been freelance writing since 1998, but after Matt's death I decided to focus my writing primarily in the addiction recovery and mental health space. I wanted to educate people and hopefully inspire them to seek treatment. In this small way, I would honor my son's memory.

By far the most healing endeavor I have engaged in since Matt's death was writing my memoir, *My 13th Station*. It was extremely difficult to reach deep into the memory jar to reconstruct the story of what happened to my son, to relive the emotions and searing pain. Surprisingly, this turned out to be cathartic in many ways. While writing the book I was able to parse through the traumatic events, one grisly moment at a time, which helped me process a lot of the residual trauma and emotions. Mostly, though, the book honors his life and his memory, while also providing useful information for other parents with a troubled teen or young adult child.

But in the end, it is my strong, unshakable Catholic faith that has kept me from spiraling down into the depths of despair. I thank God for my faith, which I consider an enormous gift and a treasure. With God's grace I believe I will eventually be reunited with my deceased loved ones, and for that unwavering belief I am truly grateful.

CHAPTER 4

Gina's Story

*M*y name is Gina Cousineau, and I am a grieving mother. Ironically, my entire life I have always wanted to be a mother. My very first memories revolved around playing with my dolls, pretending to be pregnant, and then at the age of seven, being gifted with my first living doll, my nephew Eric. My sister Lou, affectionately called Lou Lou, sixteen years my senior, was like my second momma. I spent weekends, school holidays, and summer vacations with her, and it seemed she loved my company as much as I loved hers. After Lou gave birth to Eric, I have a clear memory of him being handed to me, a seven-year-old, in the back seat of their Volkswagen Bug. I had been charged with holding him on the trip home from the hospital. My sister, a no-nonsense kind of gal, had a very strict schedule for the baby and was not breastfeeding (perhaps this would later contribute to her demise), so I was given full reign with little Eric. From baths and bottles, to strolling around the neighborhood, I got to pretend to be a mommy. And lucky for me, the next five years would bring two more babies into my life.

By the time I was in high school, I had definitely established a pretty strong personality. In fact, when I was younger, as the baby of the family by many years—with my sister, Lou, sixteen years older; my sister, Chris, fourteen years older; and my brother, Mike, six and a half years older—I was considered the "brat." That attitude continued on with me through adolescence. I even wondered if I would ever find a man who would put up with me!

From early on, I took on the role of "team mom" among my peers, even being nicknamed "Momma Regina" by them. I brought snacks, baked cookies, and planned get-togethers for my teammates on the swim team. I loved my role.

Fast forward to college. The University of California, San Diego, was where I would meet Mark, the man who would become my husband, during the second quarter of my freshman year. I was seventeen and he was nineteen. I knew within two weeks that he would be the man I would marry. I promptly tossed my dream of being an obstetrician away, knowing that I preferred to focus on building my own family.

After leaving U.C.S.D. at the end of that year, I enrolled in the local community college in San Diego and moved in with my future husband at the ripe old age of eighteen. My parents never knew we lived together. I got my associate's degree in culinary arts, and started working as a chef's apprentice for the Hilton Corporation on Mission Bay. When I had to work on Christmas Day, I suddenly realized that I could no longer pursue a career in the food industry, as that kind of schedule would never work for family life. So, I enrolled at San Diego State University to start earning my bachelor's degree in nutrition. It would not be until I finished my master's program in integrative and functional nutrition in 2019 that I would finally get to take on that "physician" type role with my clients that I had always dreamed of.

Mark and I married in 1984 on my twenty-first birthday. I could not have imagined a better way to celebrate this monumental day. We made the move to Orange County, and over the next few years, Mark established his career in environmental management while I completed my degree at California State University, Long Beach. We purchased our first home in San Clemente, and began to build our family by getting pregnant just two months into the pursuit.

Our angel, Mary, was born on June 3, 1987. I was living the dream as a stay-at-home mom at twenty-four years of age. It was at this time that I began practicing self-care with regular exercise, and participating in a prenatal/postpartum exercise program. When the program closed its doors, an idea was born. Because I had placed so much value on this experience, I partnered with another mom and opened an exercise studio called "Kicks For Two," eventually adding a retail shop. Through all these years, I struggled with what they termed "secondary infertility." Imagine being surrounded by pregnant women and babies, day in and day out, and not being able to have another child myself.

It is important to mention that life was not all blissful at this time. My big sister, Lou, my second momma and my world, had been diagnosed with breast cancer at age thirty-five when I was nineteen. We knew nothing about this disease, having no family history, and breast self-examination was just coming to the forefront of preventive care. Her cancer was advanced, but she fought hard for eleven years. It was during the latter stages of her illness that I took on the role of advocate for her, and for our family. No one else, not her husband, nor my parents or siblings, were able to make critical decisions for my sister's care.

I was thirty years old the Memorial Day weekend that we got the call that Lou was back in the hospital and it was bad. After participating in what was the first of many care conferences I would be part of in my lifetime, we learned that there was little hope for Lou. Eventually, it was I who made the decision to bring her home on hospice, and was blessed to spend most of those last few months of her life loving on her. Lou finally succumbed to the disease on September 25, 1993 at the age of forty-six. I thought my life was over when my sister passed away. I had lost the love of my life. My only solace was my daughter Mary, the angel of the world, who was there to hold my hand through what was only the first of many more tragic life experiences to come.

After seven and a half years of infertility, we were blessed on December 9th, 1994, with our son Derek, thus gifting Mary with *her* first living doll, just as I had been gifted one many years before. She doted on him and loved him like no other, and life was grand.

By this point, I realized there was no time to waste, as I was approaching thirty-five and still hoped to grow my family. So, in the true spirit of getting what I truly desired in life and advocating for myself, we eventually achieved a successful I.V.F. pregnancy. We were gifted with our beautiful babies, Alaina and Evan, on November 3, 1997.

For the next nine years, I was living the dream. After closing our fitness business soon after my sister's death, I went on to become a fitness professional, teaching group exercise classes and providing personal training sessions. It was the perfect part-time endeavor to use my nutrition education, practice my own self-care, and embrace motherhood. In raising four athletes, our family was constantly on the move. We loved our crazy, busy life.

After Lou died, I assumed the role as matriarch of the family at age thirty. We were blessed with a large extended family in the Southern

California area. My parents, who were in their early forties when I was born, were a huge part of our lives and moved to San Clemente in the early 2000s to be closer to us. The family spent all holidays and special events together, enjoying Italian food, playing games, and participating in spirited conversations.

When Evan and Alaina turned eight, I felt for the first time that I could take a breath. I was finally able to take time for a little self-care and to delve more deeply into my faith journey. I joined two Bible studies, one at my parish and the other at the Mission San Juan Capistrano. I do remember that, at this point in time, there was much tragedy going on around me. We had lost a few dads in the community, much too young, to heart conditions. I clearly remember driving on the 5 freeway northbound, going under the overpass just before the Beach Cities exit, thinking about the fact that no children in our community of peers had yet succumbed. I find I use this word, succumbed, on the regular now in my life, compelled now to look at the definition: "Fail to resist pressure, temptation, or some other negative force and/or die from the effect of a disease or injury." Deep breath.

I am not sure how much later it was, after having that reassuring thought under the freeway overpass, that our lives flipped upside down. Weeks, perhaps. As stated earlier, we were truly living the dream, raising our family in the little Spanish Village by the Sea, the beach town where my husband vacationed every August as a child with his extended family. With such wonderful memories of those times in San Clemente, it was the perfect place for us to grow a family.

I purposely kept my knowledge of what was going on in the big bad world limited, turning on the local news and perusing the newspaper only occasionally. Ironically, when I did read the paper I always read the obituaries, scanning the listings for early deaths and wanting to learn the cause (was it preventable?), and more importantly, if any children were listed in the obituaries. I kept my kids bubble wrapped and was always cognizant of the way I felt when they were all tucked safely in their beds—blessed.

Our tragedy began on a rather typical day, April 30, 2007, after dropping the kids off at swim practice in Irvine, our home away from home. I headed to the grocery store to make good use of that "quiet" time. While there, I got the call that Evan was not feeling well, so I rushed back to the pool, finding him curled in a ball, wrapped in his towel and in the arms of his coach.

I took my precious boy into my arms and tried to assess the situation. Although Derek and Alaina were still in the pool, it quickly became apparent that we needed to head right home, having no idea what was to come. About six weeks earlier, Evan had experienced what I assumed was his first migraine headache. That my boy had had a migraine was not surprising to me, since my mother, brother, Mary, and I all suffered from them. One thing we always knew, even though we felt horrific while in the midst of one, was that the migraines wouldn't kill us. I clearly remember calling the pediatrician and relaying what had happened, followed with an appointment set for the next day. In hindsight, even though there were many telltale signs that had occurred since the prior August that should have concerned us, none of these events would have given us *any* indication of what was to come.

With the kids now piled in our vehicle, Evan lay there in the back row clearly suffering. When he began to throw up, his brother Derek propelled himself back there to hold and comfort him. Then, as I pulled into the next pool to drop Derek off for water polo practice, Evan began to have an active seizure. Just as I was calling 911,

I spotted Derek's coach. I called him over to the car and implored him to go with Evan and me to the emergency room because 911 hadn't yet answered the call.

As we approached the entrance to the E.R., Evan was immediately whisked away. Once he was settled in his room, I entered to find him curled up in a ball, looking nothing like the vibrant boy he was mere hours ago. It was terrifying. At that moment in time, I had no idea that our lives would never be the same. Mark and Mary were at a banquet for the U.S.C. water polo athletes, celebrating the end of her freshman year. Derek and Alaina were on a pool deck somewhere. I felt so alone, until I wasn't. In a blink of an eye, upon hearing that Evan was sick, every person who cared about us had either joined me in his little cubicle at the E.R. or had piled into the waiting room.

After a battery of tests and hours of waiting, Evan was going to be transported to the I.C.U. at Children's Hospital, Orange County, our local children's hospital. I was forced to sit in the front of the ambulance when all I wanted was to stay at my son's side. At this point Mary had made it back to Orange County and was following the ambulance in our car. Mark and I decided it was best for him to get the other kids home and tucked safely into their beds. Oh dear God.

Speaking of God, He was not so much on my mind back then. After losing my sister Lou, I'd found it hard to pray. I had prayed and prayed for her earthly healing, but I didn't get what I wanted. So I made the decision to no longer ask for my earthly desires, as to avoid being "mad" at God for not granting them. So, I became very careful when asking something of God. I often now use the phrase "lucky or blessed" when I look at the good aspects of my life, no longer quite sure which one I am.

At the end of one of the longest days of my life, I was dragged into the conference room at C.H.O.C. along with my husband and our daughter Mary, who was just nineteen years old. The two doctors sitting across from us told us that Evan had a disease called adrenoleukodystrophy, or A.L.D. They told us very clearly that there was no treatment and no cure, that he would be dead in six to twelve months, and that his death would be horrific. As the doctors spoke, their words were seared into my memory where they will forever remain. I remember turning to Mary on one side of me and telling her she was quitting school, then turning to my husband on the other side of me and telling him he was quitting work, and that we would play with Evan until he could no longer play. That night we were left sitting there with absolutely no hope.

The next day the doctors told us that a bone marrow transplant (B.M.T.) was a possible treatment for boys with late-diagnosed A.L.D. It was at that point that my husband and I did what we did best, being advocates for our kids. He took the role of finding the most qualified doctors to help save our boy, and I took the role of figuring out how to keep Evan with us in the "here and now," and beyond. I would take control of this very uncontrollable situation—or at least I hoped I would.

The next forty-five days were a whirlwind, with the end result of getting our boy, who had now lost some of his sight and hearing capabilities, but who was cognizant as ever, to transplant. We decided to head to the University of Minnesota Children's Hospital, where their B.M.T. program for advanced A.L.D. in boys was considered the gold standard of care. Evan deserved no less. The emotional rollercoaster of these weeks is too complex and difficult to recount here. All that mattered was, during that month and a half, we now had hope.

While my relationship with my God was precarious to say the least, I did allow, or I'd say, *insist*, that He guide me through this tenuous time. For example, when we learned Evan was a candidate for transplant, and the best hope for success was with a sibling match, I told God that I would agree to Evan's transplant if one of the kids matched. No such luck; none of the kids were a match. When we were told that cord blood could save Evan, I told God He had better find a match. He found two! When we had trouble getting insurance to allow us to go to Minnesota for the treatment, I told God He had better make it happen or else Evan would not have that lifesaving transplant. Insurance finally approved it. And when we were just hours from Evan being admitted for the transplant, and things were not happening at *my* speed, I told God that if He didn't get him admitted that day, I would take Evan home. We were admitted by the end of the day. Deep breath. Thank you, God, for answering the pleas (demands) of Your bossy girl.

We walked into the children's bone marrow transplant unit on June 11, 2007. While we would be akin to prisoners in that hospital for the next five months, when I look back a most comforting memory stands out. My precious son, so sick, distressed, and unhappy upon arrival, had been excited, full of pure hope that his disease would be cured.

We lost Evan six months from the day of his diagnosis with A.L.D., on the day before he and his twin sister Alaina's tenth birthday. It was All Soul's Day, how appropriate. In the end, Mary and I bathed Evan for the last time, one of our favorite parts of our days in Minnesota. We picked out his clothes, going with a San Clemente Ocean Festival shirt, his blue warm-up pants, his blue football sweatshirt, and a new O'Neil beanie that friends sent to us. We bagged his pants so we could see his striped blue boxers hanging out in Evan fashion, and finished with his favorite socks. Then I held him. He was perfection. After everything my boy had been through, his face was peachy cream and soft as a baby's bottom, with not an indication of stress or harm. It was amazing. We all spent the next few hours taking turns holding him. I looked at him one last time, turned away from him, hugged our nurses, and walked out the door. The absolute worst thing I will ever experience in my lifetime. But I did it; Evan held my hand the entire time. My boy, the love of my life is gone, and oh how I can't wait to join him.

The agony of those months spent with Evan in the fight for his life will be embedded in my soul forever. My passion and fire for patient advocacy had begun with my own infertility journey, then through the fight for my sister's life, and now with my own son. Patient advocacy is a gift from God that I have used many times over in the years since, helping family and strangers alike, whether they wanted my intervention or not. I see it as a ministry that I take very seriously.

After losing Evan, I prayed that God would take my life. When we flew home from Minnesota on their birthday without Evan, I asked God to take the plane down and put us all out of our misery. I stopped wearing my seatbelt. As I contemplated this new life that I had no intention of being part of, God began to direct me. While I knew I had no choice but to get out of bed every day, not for myself, but for my husband and children who needed me, He also gave me a great task. God wanted me to use Evan's experience, and every patient that was in need, is in need, and will be in need, as the catalyst to educate and empower others. I was tasked with a mission to inspire people, like you and me, to recycle our bodies through blood and cord blood donation, as well as joining the bone marrow registry and the commitment to organ donation. While at that time, in my grief, I had no idea what this project would look like, I did know that without donors Evan would have had no hope. Prior to our journey with Evan, I didn't know the power the human body possessed with its recourses to help cure others in need. Now that I was informed on a very personal level, I realized this critical need. Hence the Be A Hero Become A Donor Foundation came to fruition.

Fast-forward fourteen years, and here I sit today in a friend's home in Watsonville, California, while they are on vacation, looking over the vast ocean from their loft, writing my story. I came here to be alone with my thoughts without distractions to finally put my thoughts down on paper. Indeed, I know full well that misery loves company. I also realize, though, that throughout all the tragedies in life, empires continue to be built, babies continue to be born, and people continue to die, as this is *life*. I am no different than any other grieving mother. I had to choose my own path to survive the most difficult loss a human would ever endure. The loss of my son has allowed me to see how the Blessed Mother is truly my kindred spirit. She and I watched our sons being literally tortured, and yet we somehow survived it. My salvation is the promise of Calvary, and knowing that while I would never allow my own son's suffering to be in vain, hence the founding of Evan's foundation, I would never allow Jesus's suffering to be futile either. That being said, I live a life of both joy and misery, happiness and sadness, and each and every day I get up with the goal of doing no harm, and to exude Christ-like behavior to all those I meet. I fail every single day, yet I get up again the next day, joining up with my daily rosary group, to begin anew, and to try, try again.

People often say after a great loss that it was "God's will" or it's all in "God's plan," but I refuse to submit to that way of thinking. What I do know is this . . . that my God is great and mighty and loving. He has guided me since I was a young child. I don't know why He chose me or why I have allowed Him to continue to influence me all these years. So many choose the opposite path. I also know that if you truly believe in God, you have to believe in the ugliness and evil that exists all around us, attempting to destroy us. My God did not single out my son to torture. My God did not steal from me my own flesh and blood to allow me to use my grief to do good. My God's tears flow in unison with mine, as He holds me tightly in His arms, as we mourn the loss of my perfect vibrant boy together. My God helps me to carry the very heavy cross that is part of my earthly life, which for some reason seems to grow heavier and heavier with each passing day. My God has promised paradise to all those who believe in Him. My husband and I raised our children to believe in Him, so I am confident that it is the evil in this world that attempts to divide us, to cause extreme pain in this earthly life, especially for people who stand firm in our faith. But our reward comes after our death. We simply need to keep our eye on the prize.

My life experiences, and my intense faith, have allowed me to weather the storms I had never anticipated in this life. Because of these experiences, I have become an influencer of sorts and a mentor to many. My family, friends, and clients look to me for advice on the regular, and I hand it out like candy, happy to share what I feel is a gift from my God. I don't know why He has given me this role. With this mentorship role, I am often exposed to a great deal of sadness and sorrow, and even the loss of relationships. But despite the pain and suffering I endure in this role, I will accept the losses that come with the saves. My ability to speak my mind and advocate for others has literally saved lives. I will never, ever, though, be able to do enough good works to make up for the one life I could not save, my precious Evan. But still, I continue on.

I always knew that being blessed with a grandchild would help me find true joy again, and I have. Our sweet Olivia even has the same round head and striking blue eyes as her uncle Evan. I know without a doubt that both Evan and my sister Lou handpicked Liv just for us. This child is responsible for helping to heal that hole in my heart that is etched in the shape of my son. I share about Uncle Ev with Olivia on the regular. His face is seen throughout my home and also in hers.

Evan was a precocious boy who was loved by all. With Mary being so much older, the sibling rivalry was usually amongst the youngest three, being only three years apart. Evan was the peacemaker, always attempting to keep the calm between Derek and Alaina. Everyone wanted to be friends with Evan. He was clever, handsome, vibrant, and talented. A three-sport athlete, he swam at age two, rode a two-wheeler at three, and stepped onto the roller hockey rink at four and never looked back, transitioning into ice hockey soon after. He loved the camaraderie he had with his all of his teammates no matter the sport, and they adored him. He was really perfect in every way, until the disease started to take its course. And as he met his demise, I prayed for God to take him, and that time He answered my prayers. For this I am grateful. My son is now perfect and healed in paradise. And now here I am, with one foot on this earth and one foot in Heaven, impatiently, yet patiently, waiting to be reunited with my boy again.

Along with the work I've done with the Be A Hero Become A Donor Foundation, I was also one of the three mommas who brought newborn screening for A.L.D. to fruition in California. Given we have the highest birthrate here in California, the impact we will have on the families given this horrendous diagnosis will be monumental. Had this technology existed for Evan, he would likely be a vibrant young adult today.

Even while learning to tolerate this new life I had no intention of being part of, my competitive spirit never left me. At the age of fifty, I decided to run my first half marathon. Soon after I was asked to participate in a Spartan Race with my local boot camp, and after that, being the mother and organizer that I am, I motivated a group of athletes, young and old alike, to join in the camaraderie of this racing community. Since that time, I have either been running for my life or running from my life, but one thing is for sure, I have run all over the world competing in these obstacle course events.

Since earning my master's degree, thirty years after graduating from college, I now have a fruitful business as a culinary nutritionist, where I merge my passion of health with helping others to live a long, healthy, independent, joyful life using "food as medicine." I refer to it as "Mama G's Lifestyle," through which I educate, motivate, and help people around the country change the trajectory of their lives by putting the science and evidence of wholesome food on their plates with nutritious and delicious food choices.

Between my time with our granddaughter, my lifelong commitment to my health through wholesome food and exercise, and my new business venture, life is joyful. That being said, the hole in my heart in the shape of my son Evan remains, and while I impatiently await the reunion with my perfect boy, with one foot in heaven and one on this earth, I do what I can to help others find their joy as well.

I know the temptations and pressures of the world today are very real. This is perhaps more true now than ever because of the powerful influences of the Internet and social media. I do believe that our faith will free us from the manipulations and deceptions we experience as we reveal our faith for all to see, and, unfortunately, we will be hated for it. I once read a meme that stated, "Be the kind of woman that, when your feet hit the ground each morning, the devil says, 'Oh crap, she's up.'" Evil will not win in my life, and I will continue to do everything in my earthly power to protect the people that I am blessed to encounter by role modeling Christ-like behavior and helping them carry their own crosses.

> My all-powerful Lord, You have conquered the evil one and provide all the grace I need to overcome his lies and deceptions. Open my mind to discern Your voice and give clarity to the voice of the evil one so that I may choose You with my whole heart and reject all that the evil one tries to say to me. Jesus, I trust in You.
>
> —Catholic Daily Reflections

To learn more about bone marrow and cord blood donation:
https://bahbad.org/ald/

CHAPTER 5

Jodi's Story

My name is Jodi. I grew up in the San Fernando Valley, with loving parents and two wonderful siblings. We moved to Orange County when I was twelve years old, and I just loved living by the beach. I met my husband, Bill, when I was nineteen and he had just turned twenty-one—it was love at first sight (at least for me, anyway). We dated for seven years. After we married we bought a beautiful home in Huntington Beach, CA. We lived there for two years before settling in South Orange County to the home we still reside in today.

Two years later, we had our firstborn son. He surprised us by arriving five and a half weeks before his due date. Jarrod Paul Barber was born weighing four pounds eight ounces and measuring nineteen inches long. Jarrod had lots of black hair, gorgeous blue "Paul Newman" eyes, and the most beautiful olive skin tone. The nurse immediately took Jarrod into the N.I.C.U., so my husband and I were not able to hold our baby boy right away, and that really hurt. I was nervous and scared. Jarrod was fed through a tube inside an incubator for ten days. We finally brought him home weighing just four pounds six ounces. Our tiny miracle baby was so very beautiful.

Jarrod was four when his brother Blake was born. Our little family was complete. The boys were close and, as they got older, Jarrod was very protective and always wanted to vet Blake's friends, making sure they didn't drink or do drugs.

As a young boy, Jarrod loved typical pastimes like playing with Legos and being outdoors. Growing up he played baseball for nine years, and also loved bodysurfing, skateboarding, Harry Potter, and life in general. He enjoyed being with his family and friends and was a happy kid.

I have been lucky to know what it's like to be happily married and to raise two healthy, fun-loving sons; to live in a nice upper-middle-class home; and to have dinner on the table every night. I know what it's like to go to my sons' baseball games, to enjoy family gatherings and trips, and to celebrate birthdays and holidays together. Building a happy, healthy family was always my number one purpose in life, and I knew how very blessed I was. And then, life changed.

Bill and I first discovered Jarrod was smoking marijuana when he was seventeen. We had come home from dinner and walked in on Jarrod and his friend smoking pot in his room. We sat with our son for two hours while he cried and promised us he would never do it again. During that chat he admitted he had started smoking pot when he was fourteen while at a sleepover at a friend's house. My husband and I were completely shocked.

Bad things started happening after that, each one related to his marijuana use. First his grades started slipping, and then he got in trouble at school because pot was found in his car. He was then required to attend twenty A.A. meetings, but Jarrod said the meetings "didn't relate" to him because he didn't drink.

But it was during his senior year that we noticed a change in his behavior. That year Jarrod had been injured on his dirt bike and suffered a broken collarbone, and the doctor prescribed Vicodin for the pain. Well, that was the beginning of his spiral into prescription pills. Unbeknownst to us, Jarrod began experimenting with Xanax, Adderall, and OxyContin before finally obtaining a prescription for Opana. Bill and I had no idea any of this was happening until late 2009.

It was on January 8, 2010, that our lives were shattered. That evening Jarrod was at home, sitting on the sofa and watching a movie with two friends. His dad and I said goodnight and went upstairs to bed around 11:00 pm. At around 3:00 am, my husband woke up and noticed that the hall light was still on, so he went downstairs. There he found Jarrod sitting up on the couch, barely breathing. He tried desperately to wake him and, when unable to, called me downstairs. Bill performed CPR on his son while I called 911. It was the most shocking, devastating experience we have ever witnessed. The paramedics came and worked on Jarrod some more. He was then rushed to the hospital by ambulance, with me sitting in the front seat and his dad following behind.

The doctors worked on Jarrod for about a half hour and were unable to save our son. At 3:47 am, our son was pronounced deceased. The doctor came out to tell us the news and he broke down in tears. He shared he had lost his teenage brother years back to an overdose.

We were the only ones in the E.R. waiting room. After I was told that Jarrod didn't make it, I screamed in disbelief, "No, this is where my son was born!"

We walked into the room and sat by his bed and said our tearful goodbyes. We grabbed his belongings, and then I took the necklace off him that his aunt had given him, and put it on. It was a rope with five silver rings containing the words encouragement, hope, courage, wisdom, and strength. Jarrod loved that necklace and never took it off. That night, I walked out of the hospital wearing it.

So, what led us to that point? It had been just three short months since the first visit with a doctor who convinced Jarrod and I that his cravings for marijuana and Opana would go away with the help of anti-anxiety and antidepressant medications. Prescribing benzodiazepines, without offering any counseling, to a teenager who was addicted to opioids was simply irresponsible and dangerous. That doctor had to know my son could relapse.

On Jarrod's last visit with the doctor, just two days before he died, he was handed two handfuls of samples of a drug called Seroquil. The prescription read to take three to four pills per day. Seroquil is an antipsychotic medication prescribed off-label for people who struggle with sleep problems. On January 8, 2010, Jarrod took the Seroquil (three, as prescribed) for the first time, along with clonazepam (Klonapin) and Cymbalta, which had all been prescribed by that doctor. He also crushed a quarter of Opana that night. The combination of these pills caused my son's death.

After Jarrod's death, I was in shock for a whole year. I kept expecting him to walk through the front door asking, "What's for dinner?" I even swore I heard the creaking sounds upstairs at night, just like when Jarrod walked to his bedroom. Some parents, after losing a child, will clean out their child's closet and get rid of all their clothes. They may even re-decorate the room after their child dies. Not me.

I still have his clothes in the closet and have left the room the same as the day he passed. I have, however, given some of Jarrod's clothes away to homeless boys who struggle with drugs. We all grieve differently, and that's okay. There is no right or wrong way to deal with the loss of a child. For me, though, leaving the room intact just felt right.

After losing our nineteen-year-old son to a prescription drug overdose, I asked my husband, "How did it get to this point? What the hell happened?" So many questions were swirling around in my head. I soon realized my son's death never should have happened, that it could have been prevented. This lit a spark inside me.

In the aftermath of Jarrod's death, I could have kept silent. I could have told people he died of a heart problem or just died mysteriously in his sleep. Instead, I chose to tell the truth to hopefully save another family from going through the devastation we had experienced. Helping others avoid such a loss became my true purpose and passion in life.

Not only did I lose my child in 2010, but three of Jarrod's close friends also died from overdoses. They were friendly, respectful, polite, and loving kids. I soon began hearing of more young lives lost in the same way. In Orange County, California, eighty-eight young lives were cut short by overdoses that year. Sadly, the numbers continued to increase.

Oxymorphone (Opana) had been in my son's system the night he passed away. Jarrod's friends told me about a physician, Dr. Lisa Tseng, who was over-prescribing opioids and other medications to several of their friends. Her business card was in Jarrod's wallet.

Jarrod had become addicted to Opana, which Tseng was prescribing to teens in bottles of ninety pills. Yes, it was my son's choice, but she was the doctor. Of course, Tseng knew these kids didn't have terminal cancer, the use for which this drug was developed.

I knew with every fiber of my being that this information must be exposed to the public to stop this person from harming more lives. I called a newspaper and got an article published. I also began collecting empty pill bottles from other moms whose teens were taking pills prescribed by Dr. Tseng and took them to the Drug Enforcement Administration. I soon discovered that people of all ages were driving forty-five miles, even a hundred miles, to wait in line at Dr. Tseng's office for their fix.

Today, Dr. Lisa Tseng is in prison, facing a sentence of thirty years to life, on three counts of second-degree murder and twenty-one counts of reckless prescribing. I hope her sentence puts every physician on notice and encourages them to think twice each time they prescribe a medication for a patient. These dirty doctors who have been recklessly prescribing addictive pills, driven by greed, will eventually be convicted.

My new mission in life began to unfold during the first year after Jarrod's death. First, I was asked to speak in a high school health class. I asked Cole, a young man who was clean from addiction, to come along. His story really resonated with those teens, and I realized we needed to speak out and share our stories to more students. I continue to work together with a couple of young adults, speaking at schools and informing kids wherever we can.

I have driven in the dark of night to help persuade addicted young people into getting treatment. I am invited into family homes to assist with interventions. I drive to motels and pick up struggling addicts and drive them to detox. I try to locate scholarships to help get young people into treatment. I am not a professional, but I'm a mother who lost her son. I know my son's death was preventable and will do whatever I can to prevent other families from going through such a devastating loss.

When someone asks for help, they should be able to receive it immediately! Sadly, this is seldom the case. The majority of people who call for help cannot afford insurance. It is my belief that we, as a society, need to advocate for affordable insurance coverage for long-term treatment, as well as funding for aftercare programs. Thirty days, even sixty days, is simply not long enough to break the addiction cycle. It takes about two years for the brain to heal from an addiction.

I post on my social media accounts every time I hear about another overdose death. Some weeks I have posted about two or even three young lives lost locally to addiction. As sad as these messages are, the public needs to be informed, and most *want* to be informed. But the message of hope is just as important, so I also post the success stories. As long as you or your loved one is walking, talking, and breathing, there is hope!

In 2011, I went to local businesses and put up posters emblazoned with the faces of twenty-one children who had overdosed and died. Each poster included my phone number and an open invitation to call. The calls poured in. One call was from a mother named Christine Wood who said she would help me in any way she could. We decided together that Red Ribbon Week, a drug prevention awareness campaign observed in our schools each October, simply wasn't enough. We were driven to go a step further, so together we produced a short documentary entitled *Overtaken*.

As a result, my mission quickly expanded nationwide. We mailed *Overtaken* to rehabs, sober living homes, courtrooms, and schools. My hope was that eventually *Overtaken* and its accompanying lesson plan would become part of the health curriculum in every school across the country.

In the film, high school athletes, cheerleaders, straight-A students, college students, and my young friend, Cole, relate their heartbreaking stories of addiction. Some continue to speak as mentors before thousands of students, proud to be giving back and helping others.

One of my goals is to end the stigma that surrounds addiction. The stigma, and the silence, is killing thousands of lives. Opioid addiction can happen to anyone at any age. All it takes is a broken bone and a doctor's prescription for pain medication.

Our family's story has been featured in newspapers and magazines, on the news and radio, and on several talk shows, including *Dr. Drew* and *Dr. Oz.* as well as featured in books, such as *Generation Rx* and *The Addict Among Us*. ABC aired two public service announcements that I produced, and I had a billboard erected on the busy I-5 freeway in Orange County to raise awareness. Two local cities approved a plaque, memorial tree, and sculpture to honor our loved ones who were lost to overdose, as well as to spread awareness and open up the dialogue between parents and kids. My hope is to have this repeated in several more cities.

I spoke before the California Senate about the *Controlled Substance Utilization Review and Evaluation System* (CURES) funding bill, and rallied with other parents on the Capitol steps. I later told my story to the California Medical Board to encourage the passing of the CURES bill. In Washington, D.C., I joined thousands of people holding signs and marching to the White House in memory of loved ones lost to addiction. After that, I organized another rally here in our hometown.

I collected signatures for *The Good Samaritan Law*, which offers legal protection for people who give reasonable assistance to those who are, or who they believe to be, injured, ill, in peril, or otherwise incapacitated. I was also honored to receive letters of recognition from the offices of President Obama and President Trump.

I am certainly joined by many other concerned citizens and grieving parents in making these efforts. There are several great organizations, such as FED Up, Mothers Against Prescription Drug Abuse (MAPDA), and Shatterproof to name a few, and hundreds of parents advocating for people who struggle with addiction. They are working very hard to get more funding directed toward treatment of any type, easy and affordable access to long-term treatment, naloxone (Narcan) distribution, funding for the Medication Assisted Treatment Program (M.A.T.), and for more readily available resources to combat substance use disorders. We want the government to consider *this* epidemic to be just as important as the current COVID-19 pandemic.

These days, my phone rings constantly with news of overdose deaths or requests for help. Sadly, the epidemic has worsened. Across the U.S., the deadly fentanyl has been implicated in the loss of even more young lives. Fentanyl is a synthetic opioid that is fifty to a hundred times more potent than morphine. It is being found in counterfeit pills, such as Xanax, and OxyContin, and also in the heroin, meth, and cocaine supplies purchased on the street.

Young people are dying *every single day*. Addiction can happen at any age, in any home. Substance abuse and addiction affect people from all walks of life. This is why I feel a sense of urgency to educate everyone we can. Inform yourselves and attend events in your area to learn about this growing epidemic and about the new synthetic drugs that are easily accessible to our children online. We must reach young people *before* they start experimenting. Talk to your children at an early age and don't stop talking. Drug test your kids and get involved. If I knew then what I know now, maybe my son would still be alive.

I hope to inspire you to take a stand and join me, and thousands of other grieving mothers, in the fight against the number one cause of accidental deaths in the United States. We must come together as a whole; it truly takes a village to bring about change. Together, we *can* make a difference.

This mission, this new purpose, is how I have coped over the years. My advice for parents who have lost a child is do what you can to survive. This can mean counseling, praying, taking yoga classes, or daily walks. Understand that your child is with God and with you spiritually, watching over you, smiling down at you. Know that it is perfectly normal to be laughing one minute and the next minute crying your eyes out. If you have other children, know that they need you, your spouse does too, and they all want to see you happy.

Oh, but the triggers! It still kills me when seeing parents on the beach with their two sons, or driving by the ball field where Jarrod played baseball all those years. Hearing his favorite Hip Hop songs on the radio or seeing his favorite movies shown on T.V. brings me right to tears. The list goes on. These triggers make me smile and want to cry at the same time.

Today, both my missions are clear. I balance my efforts to save lives with staying happy and grateful that I have my supportive husband of thirty-five years by my side, and our delightful son, Blake, who works as a tennis coach. Blake teaches me every day that life can still be fun. He reminds me we are only here for a short time and need to make the most of this precious life. He continues to experience what he calls "waves of emotions," which is normal and healthy.

But I still, and always will, have days where I just long for my son's hug. Where I want to hear his voice and his laugh. Where I miss hearing him say to a friend, "Oh, whuuttt?" I sometimes get a pain in my gut that is hard to explain. I have questions running through my mind, wondering where would Jarrod be today if he was still alive? Would he be clean, off drugs? Would he still be struggling or in jail? Would he be married and working in a successful career?

Thankfully, Jarrod appears to us in different ways, bringing us peace and putting smiles on our faces. We know that even though he is with God, he is still with us spiritually, so please don't ever kill a "bee!" I say that because on the day my son passed away, his brother held a vigil on the corner for friends to sign posters as a way of expressing grief. A bee landed on one of the posters and stayed there all day long. The next morning we walked over to pick up the posters and the bee was still there, alive, and then flew away. Well, why bees? Because I am a florist! Soon the bees began to appear numerous times in our home, inside our cars, on top of our cars, and even landing on us. Bees were everywhere, and there have been plenty of other spiritual encounters that occurred over the years. These signs bring me comfort, telling me that Jarrod is in God's hands, that he is okay, and that he will always be here with us.

Here are a few of my articles and video links if you would like to get to know more about my mission:

- Overtaken documentary: https://www.youtube.com/watch?v=e9oj3E-NPtI
- Overtaken 2: https://www.youtube.com/watch?v=SdwpYsPCJuU&t=52s
- Orange Coast Magazine: https://www.orangecoast.com/features/doses-reality/
- Orange County Register: https://www.ocregister.com/2011/03/14/fatal-overdoses-were-fueled-by-prescription-drugs/
- Fox 11 News: https://www.foxla.com/news/orange-county-families-fight-to-save-lives-week-of-overdose-awareness-day
- Orange County Register: https://www.ocregister.com/2011/12/04/the-worst-reality-show-in-oc/

You may find links to important resources on Jodi Barber's website:
www.overtakenlives.org

CHAPTER 6
Carmen's Story

*M*y name is Carmen, and I would like to share the story of my son, Gary.

It was the week of September 20, 2014, the nineteenth year since my husband's passing, and for some reason I was overcome with a need to have my kids and grandkids with me. I felt like a mother hen who desperately needed to gather her chicks and hold them close. In all those years, I had never asked that of my kids before, but somehow this year a deep need to have them near me tugged at my heart. I initially wanted to have a barbeque that Saturday; however, my grandson had a game that day so we made plans to get together on Sunday instead.

Gary, my twenty-five-year-old son, being his usual thoughtful self, knew I was feeling sad. So, he invited Karysa (his youngest sister) and me to join him and his fiancée, Aly, at a Galaxy soccer game on

Saturday, and then the whole family would still be able to gather together on Sunday. He planned to see his friends that Saturday morning to play football, and then meet up with us at his place in the afternoon so we could go to the Galaxy game together.

I can't explain the feeling, but something that day felt amiss. Every September 20th we do a coast-to-coast toast to his dad's memory, who was also named Gary, all of us toasting together at the same time from our locations. Karysa and I did the toast together at home, and then prepared to meet up with Gary at his house. At around 4:30 pm, I received a call from Aly. She said that Gary had not been responding to her texts. My heart dropped. I asked if he'd gone to play football with the guys, and she replied that he had never shown up.

I could hear the panic in her voice. I suggested we just meet up as planned, and Karysa and I headed out the door. Once we got on the freeway, I called Gary's phone, but still there was no answer. When I tried again, a lady answered and identified herself as a nurse from Western Medical Center. Before she could finish, I said, "I know who you are. Is my son there and is he alive?"

My heart instantly began pounding and tears started rolling down my face. My son, you see, was under my Kaiser insurance plan. Because I had worked for Kaiser for many years, I knew immediately that this situation was dire or he would have been taken to a Kaiser facility, not a trauma center. She responded that he was alive and in the I.C.U. I drove as fast as I could, trying hard to keep calm. I was shaking and just kept saying, "Oh my God, Oh my God!" I called Aly and told her where he was and that I was already on my way.

Apparently, Gary had been in a bicycle accident. He was thrown from his bike and landed in the middle of the street. He suffered from traumatic brain injuries. He had bled so much that at first they had not detected a second brain bleed, so he ended up in surgery again. There was nothing we could do but wait to see if the swelling in his brain went down.

This accident happened exactly nineteen years after his dad's passing. If the neurosurgeon had not done emergency surgery, Gary would have died on the same date as his Dad. It was crazy! Now, in hindsight, it makes sense to me why I needed my kids together on that day. I think perhaps I knew without knowing that something was going to happen.

When I walked into his room, tears flowed down my face. My beautiful son was in an induced coma and had already been through brain surgery. I wanted to scream, to cry from the deepest part of my soul! My heart was breaking into a million pieces! How could this be? How? My legs were weak; I was devastated and wanted to fall to his side and hold him, but we were told we could not, as touch could stimulate the brain and this was to be avoided.

Looking into his eyes, I could still see him there; a flicker of light still shone. Somehow, the mom in me knew I could *not* fall apart. He had only me to count on. So, I spoke with all the doctors and gathered as much information as I could to try to make the best decisions possible. It was like I went into autopilot. Perhaps it was all those years working in the E.R., or perhaps it was just the mom in me knowing she had to be strong. In the midst of all this craziness, I would have to make many personal decisions as well as the medical decisions.

The feeling of helplessness was immense. How could I not protect my son, how could I not save him, how could I not make him better? I was determined to make sure he had the best and kindest nurses taking care of him. I kept all lines of communication open and befriended as many people as I could in order to have good rapport with hospital staff and attain the very best care Gary could possibly receive. One nurse was kind of rough with him, so I spoke with the charge nurse and requested that she no longer take care of my son, which was soon handled.

It was grueling to see Gary like this. His intracranial pressures were high; they were low; he blinked; he moved; it was involuntary movement, or it was him giving us a sign. It was sheer agony being on this daily roller coaster. It felt surreal seeing him like that and knowing how much trauma he had sustained to his brain, yet his body was perfectly intact. Everyone kept saying what nice feet he had and I kept kissing his feet. I had to chuckle, thinking he'd be saying, "That's so gross, Mom!"

I felt like this could not be happening, that the whole scene was unbelievable. I had to believe he was going to survive. I have always had faith and, boy, did I have to cling to that faith then! I would have gladly traded places with him without a second thought. This was my son, the boy who came from my womb, the one who said he'd take care of me when I am old. He was like a little man from the time he was born, the brother with the answers and the glue that held us together.

The hospital at one point had so many of our friends visiting that they had to temporarily close visitation to others in the hospital. Family and friends gathered and slept wherever there was space. The amount of love that was shown to Gary was incredible. One nurse showed me a room of another patient (with patient family permission) so I could see how they decorated her room with positive sayings and pictures. I prayed for this sweet lady and her family, as she, too, was in a coma. I showed his friends the pictures of her walls and they dispersed only to come back with all the things needed to make signs and posters. His siblings did the same, and soon Gary's room was covered with signs of love!

One of his friends was able to contact the Galaxy and tell them about Gary and how much he loved soccer and the Galaxy team. In a couple days, a FedEx package arrived with a Galaxy shirt covered with all the players' signatures. Landon Donovan even sent a video of encouragement and healing for Gary. The hospital swarmed with Gary Love! It was like a crusade of love.

Friends visited daily, bringing Starbucks, some gardenias in a baggie for me to smell, toiletries, meals, and snacks. We had so much food that we started sharing it with other families and staff. People brought holy water from Lourdes and some anointing oils. There were so many gifts that sometimes we didn't even know where they had come from. I considered us very lucky to have so much support and love. My bosses from Kaiser came and asked what I needed to be able to continue paying my bills. They rallied the doctors and staff, gathering enough donations to make sure my family would not suffer financially.

Every day we received unexpected blessings. And even though I was going through this tremendously difficult time, I knew in that moment to be grateful. I prayed to God for my son and also gave thanks for all the blessings of love. When the nurses had a change of shift, we'd be asked to leave the room. Many times I'd walk the hallways and pray for others in the I.C.U. and their families. I felt that no one should have to suffer like this and that everyone there had a family who loved them—whose hearts were also breaking.

In spite of all the pain and sadness, tears and prayers, there were many funny moments, too. One was when my daughter, Deanna, asked for surgical masks and then had her kids draw silly faces on them. They were sleeping in the visitors lobby with these masks pulled up over their eyes and were such a funny sight. I also joked with the case manager when she let us use the shower, saying that we must be pretty stinky and that people had surely complained by then. These little funny moments helped keep us sane.

The number of people coming and going did get overwhelming at times. I was caught between wanting to tell everyone to leave, and asking myself what Gary would want. I knew he was close to Aly's family, and since they were getting married, this too would be his family. His closest friends were like family as well.

Since so many people wanted updates on Gary, his sister Karysa decided to start a Facebook page to undertake the difficult task of keeping everyone updated on his status. At one point Gary had over forty thousand people praying for him from all over the world, having learned about his battle. It was amazing. I was often moved to tears reading these loving and inspiring messages from so many people. That experience has left a light in my heart that confirms what I have always believed, that most humans are compassionate, loving, and kind.

It is hard to describe this journey. Life was kind of a blur and nothing else mattered other than being there for Gary and keeping things in order. I don't recall exactly how long after we were there that Aly's parents brought a motorhome to the hospital grounds so we could have a place to nap and shower. They brought food every night and fed us well. My family, Aly's family, and friends showered us with so much love and support.

One day, my friend Jim came by and literally made me go outside to get some fresh air and coffee. Before I agreed, I had him promise to make it quick, but even still he had to push me to go outside. While we were out talking in front of the hospital, a hummingbird hovered in front of us for about a minute. It just looked straight at us. It was so weird! The minute seemed like forever. This was so odd that I looked up the meaning of hummingbirds. What I found is that they represent joy, happiness, positive energy, enjoyment of life and the simple things. They also represent eternity. They are the only bird that moves its wings in the pattern of the figure eight, which is the symbol for eternity. It is also said that the hummingbird is a healer or spirit sent to help people, and is seen as a messenger from heaven.

This was pretty incredible and this little creature continues to show up in our lives. I believe it was a sign of hope, joy, and eternal life. It is said that the symbolism they represent for death is that the one who departed is happy so we should be, too. These little heavenly messengers have shown up while we (our family) are speaking of Gary, have appeared to friends when *they* were speaking of Gary, and have come around when I need confirmation that he is still around. It sounds crazy but it's true. I choose to believe the hummingbird presented itself to us to let us know Gary would be surrounded by joy and peace, and would live eternally.

Gary was admitted on September 20, 2014 to Western Medical center, and by October 7th there was no improvement. The neurosurgeon had asked permission to discuss his case with other neurosurgeons and so had reached out to get other opinions. Unfortunately, they all had the same opinion, that his brain had suffered too much trauma to recover. The neurosurgeon stated that if he had been wearing a helmet, his injuries would not have been fatal. This planted a seed in my brain.

The nurses were begging us, with tears streaming down their faces, to let him go. The doctors gave us a choice: To let him go and withdraw life support, or they would insert a feeding tube and transfer him to a skilled nursing home. Neither choice sounded good to me.

Since I had worked for Kaiser for so long, I knew all the phone numbers by heart and I placed a call to our repatriation center (E.P.RP.) and asked to speak with a doctor. Lucky for me, it was Dr. Mitts who picked up. I had worked with Dr. Mitts over the phone for years while coordinating transfers and had built a great rapport. I told her who I was, and explained that they were overseeing my son Gary Lofgren's case, and were now asking me to make a decision that I was not ready to make. Without hesitation she said, "Lets bring him home." So, on the evening of October 7th, we transferred Gary from Western Medical Center to Kaiser Hospital Anaheim's I.C.U.

Her words will forever ring in my ears. I just could not make a decision at the time. I needed more time; I needed my doctors to offer their opinions. I needed to hold my son longer, to love him just a little more. I was so blessed and grateful that Dr. Mitts was so compassionate and responded as she did. I seriously don't know how I kept my composure or how I even thought to call E.P.R.P. myself. Kaiser was like my home away from home, as I had worked twelve-hour shifts for many years there. Bringing Gary home to Kaiser was the right thing to do.

As I was walking toward Gary's new room at Kaiser, I noticed a couch in the next room that was a little bigger than the one in his room, and a nurse caught me looking at it. Soon the crew was moving Gary into this larger room. The larger couch would be easier for Aly and me to share, and the bathroom with a shower would be handy. They knew I wasn't leaving my son.

The entire Kaiser team was so kind and compassionate. Our room was always full of family and friends. Our family treasured this time and spent it loving him, taking care of him, holding his hand, and playing music for him. We prayed and prayed along with thousands of other people. There was a special novena at the church for him, and priests came by to pray for him. We wanted a miracle so badly.

But after more testing and consulting with many specialists, the result was the same. They said his brain was severely damaged and even if by some miracle he were to wake up, he would be in a vegetative state. I couldn't imagine him living like that. And if by chance he did know what was going on, how could I choose to keep him trapped in his own mind and body?

It was so strange—all this going on while *life* also went on. We celebrated my son Richard's birthday in the hospital, my daughter

Deanna brought in her chocolates and assembled her chocolate grams for her work crew there, and Aly went back and forth to school each day. There we were, day after day, living our lives under these odd conditions.

My sister arrived from Arkansas and, although this was such a sad and tragic moment in our lives, she managed to bring light and laughter to our days. I remember one of Aly's brothers found a shoe in the parking lot and nonchalantly picked it up and brought it to the room. He saw the shoe and figured it was hers because "Who else's could it be?"

Things that happened ranged from silly to heartwarming to absolutely ridiculous. One of the ridiculous moments was when the discharge planner walked in dressed to a T, hair done with just the perfect curls, and with makeup and nails that looked professionally done. After she left, my daughter and Aly made cracks about the nerve of her walking in looking so good. They said it should be a rule that these administrators come in wearing sweats, no makeup, and looking terrible—just like us. It was funny at the time, and is still funny now to imagine how one could even think about something as trivial as that in those tragic moments. But it was those ridiculous and funny moments that bonded us together and helped us get through it.

Gary and all of us were at Kaiser for a total of thirteen days. During this time, we were visited often by the doctors that were taking care of him, as well as by other doctors who knew me from my Kaiser days and who came just to offer support. I spoke to some of the doctors on a more personal level about our options, and one shared his own story about his parents and the decisions they had to make. He left me with some very powerful words, which I cling to daily. He said, "Whatever choice you make, do not look back." He told me I would only torture myself if I did. He reminded me that I just had to make the best choice for Gary and our family. I do look back at times and it is torturous! Then I remind myself of his words, and of all the confirmations I have had since then, and feel at peace.

About a week later, it became clear there was no hope for a positive outcome, so the doctors wanted to move him to a medical floor and put him on comfort measures. This meant either to insert a feeding tube and send him to a skilled nursing facility or to remove the ventilator that was keeping him alive. I didn't want to leave the I.C.U. where we had already become familiar with the nurses, so I begged them to let us stay a little longer. Thankfully, they did.

We had a family meeting and it was clear that we were all on the same page. Gary would not want to live as a vegetable in a skilled nursing facility. I did not want him to die on the 20th, as that day represented his dad's death and his bike accident, and I did not want him to pass away on his brother's birthday, which was October 18th. So, I decided that the 19th of October would be the day. How crazy and cruel is it that a mother has to pick the date of death for her child?

We announced on Facebook what was going on and asked for prayers. I didn't know it at the time, but as soon as people heard this news, a prayer vigil was arranged for Gary. On October 19th, the outside area below his room was filled with people wearing "GarBear" shirts and holding candles. Surges of love amid surges of immense pain emanated up from the gathering. Although I still prayed for a miracle, God had decided it was his time. But Gary's heart was strong, so God's plan did not include him passing on the 19th.

My poor son, and my whole family, was suffering so much. My baby would soon be physically leaving us forever. Once again I had that overwhelming feeling to kick everyone out of Gary's room. I just wanted to lie with him and hold him in my arms. However, I decided it was the right thing to allow those closest to him to say their goodbyes, so each person got five minutes alone with Gary. I did this because I felt this was what he would want. He was so very loved.

I told the doctor I did not want my son to feel any pain, and she assured me she'd give him enough medicine to make that possible. Even after the extubation took place, Gary's strong heart fought to keep beating. That moment was excruciatingly painful! The harsh reality of removing the breathing tube was that we had put an end to the possibility for a miracle to occur. I'd no longer be able to feel his heartbeat, hold his warm hand, kiss his beautiful face, or hold him in my arms. Not only would I be left with my own broken heart, but I'd also be left with the broken hearts of his siblings, nieces, and nephew. There was a moment when I looked into his eyes and I knew he was gone. His heart was still beating but I believed his soul had already soared up to heaven.

As I looked out his window, I was overcome with emotion and overwhelmed by the outpouring of love! I looked back at my son gasping for breaths as the tubes keeping him alive were now gone. One deep breath in, one quick exhale out, long pause, one deep breath in, quick exhale out, long pause, one deep breath in; it continued. Every time he exhaled we thought that was his last, and then he'd take another deep breath. For a microsecond I thought maybe God would give us our miracle after all.

This went on for hours into the next day. I felt horrible for him and I prayed he was not suffering. I spoke with the doctor and asked if she could increase his medicine so he would not suffer. She told me she'd give him the most she could. Our immediate family was gathered together in the room. Along with me were his siblings Deanna, Karysa, Richard, his fiancée Aly, and my mom. We played music for him, we prayed, we talked, we laughed, we cried, but most of all we just loved him. Gary would continue this labored breathing pattern through the night. He went to heaven on October 20, 2014, at 7:45 pm.

My daughter looked at the monitor and it showed a straight line, no heartbeat; he was really gone. We held hands and prayed and we did not want to leave. There was a core group of people that were there consistently, if not daily, right there beside our immediate family. They had become what we affectionately called our "hospital family." After we said our goodbyes for the umpteenth time, we were told they had to take his body to the morgue. Everyone started collecting items to take with them as a memento, like taking a piece of that moment with them—a blanket, a pillow, a rock from the planter. As we gathered ourselves together, we walked out a group bound like glue by this tragedy. We felt like the kids from *The Breakfast Club*, forever changed, and connected for life.

In the end our family became closer, stronger, more compassionate, more grateful, and more faithful than we could ever imagine. We did not get our miracle, yet we had experienced so many other miracles that in that moment we were fully aware and thankful. We became a tight circle, grateful for the smallest of gestures, aware of the connection between nature and God, and having a fuller knowledge of the existence of eternity and the greater meaning of life.

Because of Gary's loving heart, I had become a better person. I immediately knew his death would not be in vain and this propelled me to make something good arise from of this tragedy. On October 27th, one week after his passing, I made a note in my phone. It read, "I will not let grief overcome me! I will take care of myself and do positive things, do things to carry on Gary's legacy." You see, my son had said *he* wanted to make a difference in this world, but now I realized it would be up to me to make that happen.

For a while I was like a runaway train, with all my energy going toward making sure that, through me, he made that difference. I went on two missionary trips in Gary's honor, as he had made those trips when he was younger and he wanted to continue doing that work. I also traveled to Italy in hopes of doing some service there in his honor. Although it did not work out as planned, I was able to share his story, share his love, and donate to a couple of great causes there in his name. While in Italy, I was able to attend a special mass for Christian Unity Week and also meet up with the pastors I had been communicating with—even getting an audience with Pope Francis. I started raising awareness for helmet use, beginning with producing a public service announcement video that I eventually shared at five high schools, a church, a junior high school, and other venues.

I was invited to be a keynote speaker at a Kaiser event. The C.E.O. of Kaiser interviewed me and started a helmet awareness program after I told him I wanted help raise nationwide awareness. I was invited to be a guest on KFI talk radio, and was also interviewed by a reporter for the Orange County Register. I spoke about bike helmet safety at an event for the Anaheim Fire and Rescue, and most recently I donated over two hundred helmets to the Tustin Police Department for their community programs for helmet use. I still feel I have not done enough, yet I sometimes do feel like I am running out of steam.

The most important thing is that I am here. I am standing; I am stronger; I have love in my heart and I have loved ones that still need me now. There have been some dark days but I choose to find light and joy like the hummingbird. I know without a doubt in my heart that he lives on in another plane. You can call it spirit or energy but whatever it is, it lives on. I find that I'm more aware of nature and its magnificent beauty and I think that is where our spirit or energy goes. I thrive on the energy it gives me; it fills my heart and soul.

It's so important to remember there is no right or wrong way to grieve; time may teach us how to cope but it never diminishes our pain. We who survived the loss still want to hear stories about our loved ones because it keeps them alive, and that is a beautiful thing. It's important to share about the experience of loss, as I have found that by sharing we find connection.

If you have lost a child, you have gone through the ultimate test of all time. If you have survived that then you are stronger than you know. When things happen in my life and I get overwhelmed, I think to myself that I've gone through the worst and I can now handle anything else. Surround yourself with good people and lots of love. Love is everything . . . and it is eternal.

CHAPTER 7

Sharon "Sam's" Story

"My child died but she does not belong "in the past" and I won't "move on" from her because she lives within me. In the present. We are one in this moment and the next. Bringing her with me is the only way I can continue to exist."

—Dr. Joanne Cacciatore

My name is Sharon "Sam" Randlett Major. This is the story of my daughter,

Megan "Mia" Lauren Major,
2/23/1980 ~3/8/2011. Forever 31.

I awoke to the sound of what I thought was Mia coming in the front door. I looked at the clock and it was around 12:00 midnight. I rolled over and whispered to my husband, David, that Mia had come over again to sleep in the downstairs guest room. He gently groaned, "Yes." She was prone to insomnia and would stay up late and then decide to walk over to our house with her dog, Mikayla, when she was feeling lonely, which happened a lot. I always left the front porch light on for her, just in case. But the next morning when I went to check on her, the guest room was empty, the bed never slept in. At first, I thought I must have been dreaming.

That morning I was working on preparing our taxes, something I loathed doing but, nonetheless, had to take care of. I was sitting there at my desk deep in thought when the phone rang. When I answered I was startled to hear my son, Kyle, screaming in my ear, "Mom, Megan is gone!" I asked, "What do you mean she's gone?" I think I even asked, "Where did she go?" But deep in the pit of my stomach, I knew what he was trying to tell me, I just did not want to believe it. Kyle continued crying out, "She has died, Mom! She is dead!" After learning that he was there at her apartment, I numbly gathered my purse and keys and drove the few miles over to her place.

I arrived to find a large crowd gathered outside her apartment in the parking lot, including police officers and the coroner's van. I found Kyle and we attempted to comfort each other before he suddenly ran to the bushes to vomit. I wanted to wrap my arms around my son and comfort him, as he was violently ill. There were two women who identified themselves as grief counselors who assisted the police department, and asked if they could be of assistance. But all I wanted was to go inside Mia's apartment and talk to the police. Everyone was telling me not to, especially my son who was basically screaming at me, saying that I "couldn't see her, not like that!" Just then a police officer walked over to me and asked if I was Megan's mom. He said the coroner was with her and he highly recommended that I not go in, that the coroner would come out and speak with me when she was done. As he spoke, I was frantically wondering how I was going to tell my husband that our daughter had died.

Even though I might have appeared calm on the outside, I could feel the panicky feelings building up in my stomach, my heart, and my brain, and literally felt I was about to explode in pain. My heart was beating so fast, and I felt a knot growing in my stomach. I don't know why, but I then called our family physician to tell the office what had happened, and requested a prescription for medication.

As soon as I hung up with my doctor's office, I witnessed something I will never ever forget, my daughter's body being wheeled out on a stretcher in a dark burgundy body bag. With the morning sun shining on it, it looked like soft velvet. I wanted to touch it. I wanted to unzip the velvet bag and hold her hand, caress her beautiful golden hair, hug my beautiful blue-eyed girl just one last time. It haunts me to this day that I didn't get to say goodbye, and at that moment I didn't even think to ask.

The coroner walked over to me and offered her condolences. I expressed to her that I was a nurse and wanted details. All she could offer was that she wasn't certain of the time of death, but that Mia might have been dead for a day or longer as her body had started to decompose due to the heated apartment. She had been found on the floor near the couch where she had probably curled up to go to sleep. Lastly, the coroner stated it was probably an accidental overdose. An accidental overdose? Of what? Alcohol? Other drugs? She said the coroner's office would be performing an autopsy and would send us their findings. In the end we would learn that Megan died from an accidental overdose of alcohol.

Unbeknownst to me, our doctor had called my husband to offer his condolences on our daughter's death, when here I had been doing all I could to try to protect him from the devastating news. David showed up at the scene next.

This is not how I had imagined my life turning out. I grew up the oldest of four girls. Born in Southern California, I had what most would consider a pretty normal life. My parents raised us girls in the Lutheran faith and I was expected to always set a good example for my younger sisters in all I did. Being the oldest, I was taught to be the responsible one. While in junior high, when my mom worked full-time, I would come home, do my homework, look after my sisters, help them with their homework, and then start dinner.

When I was allowed to start dating and driving at age sixteen, I was a "rule follower," always coming home when I was told. We grew up being allowed an occasional taste of mom or dad's glass of wine or beer. As a teen, I remember my parents started to have marital issues and my dad coming home after being out drinking. I would be the one to help him to bed sometimes, not thinking anything was wrong with this, that this was normal in all families. Little did I know that, as a grown woman and mother myself, I would learn more than I ever wanted to know about the disease of alcoholism and how it would ultimately affect my own family.

"Mija," or my daughter, "Mia," had an aura about her. Even when she was struggling with her disease, she could still bring out the best in other people. Her laughter was full of lightness. She had a kind soul with a heart that was as large as her pain. She was a gift from God, loaned to me for a short thirty-one years.

I knew when I was pregnant with her that she was going to have a mind of her own. My due date was 2/8/1980, but she did not make her arrival until fifteen days later. We were having a severe weather system with flooding in San Diego County, and that year had had the most rain on record since 1872. The golf course where my husband worked was located in the Rancho Santa Fe Valley. Much of his turf equipment from the maintenance building had been lost, literally swept away in the San Dieguito River to the Pacific Ocean. I kept saying she wasn't coming into this world until the storm subsided. So naturally, when I went into labor, David didn't call my doctor. Instead, he called the weather service to make sure we could get to the hospital in La Jolla, California, where she would be born.

While in labor the entire day on February 22nd, we whiled away the hours watching the "Miracle on Ice" hockey event when the USA beat the Soviet Union during the 1980 Winter Olympics in Lake Placid, New York. Little did we know that our child would later play ice and roller hockey herself. Mia was a born athlete. Those genes definitely came from her paternal grandmother, Betty Jo, who was the captain on her high school basketball team. Megan's dad called her the "Phil Laimbeer" of her high school basketball team that he coached, due to her physical defensive style. She later exhibited this same style as a water polo player, which she lettered in during high school. Finally, early the next morning on February 23, 1980, we would welcome our beautiful blue-eyed girl into this world.

Growing up, she was sharp, smart, mischievous and quite the prankster. She was so witty and had the best timing. One of her nicknames, in addition to Mia, was "Minkie," after her Chinese zodiac personality of the Monkey. In first grade, she decided she was now going to be called by her middle name, Lauren, instead of Megan. She informed her teacher, Mrs. Penner, and her friends that her new name was Lauren. Mrs. Penner was one of her favorite teachers and humored her until Mia eventually grew tired of her new name and moved on to bigger and better things.

When Megan was eight years old, she phoned in to the local San Diego radio station Y95 FM while home sick from school one day. The radio producer, Little Tommy, and deejays, Jeff & Jer, got a kick out of her. Then when she called back a second time to talk to them, they hired her as their Monday Morning Hollywood "Showbiz" reporter. They would send her the script and she would call in from home before she left for school. One morning, she told them she wanted to do the report in her Texas accent. We didn't even know she had a Texas accent! They called her their "Meganmeister." Her signature sign-off was from Casey Kasem, the famous disc jockey from the American Top 40: "Keep your feet on the ground and keep reaching for the stars." I'll never forget her enthusiastic, "Yeah baby, back to Jeff and Jer." Remember, she was eight.

Mia excelled in her advanced placement classes during high school, especially English literature and creative writing. I am blessed to still have a collection of her journals and short stories. She was also an exceptional artist and loved using watercolor. She painted landscape paintings of her dad's golf course and the beach where she loved to spend time. She made me homemade cards, jewelry, and wrote poetry for me. I miss her every single day.

My daughter's struggles with alcoholism, drug experimentation, cutting, and depression started in her teens. Even with counseling for depression and social anxiety, and completing professional rehab programs, she could not overcome her abuse of alcohol. She struggled to stay clean longer than three months. She married her high school sweetheart at a young age and wanted to be a mom more than anything. After a series of miscarriages and then marital separation, she seemed to all but give up on life and love. I felt hopeless not being able to save her from despair.

Mia asked me to attend an A.A. meeting with her for the first time around 2003. That is where I also learned about Al-Anon. Like most people with an alcoholic loved one, I first thought Al-Anon would give me the information I needed to help my daughter stop drinking. Unfortunately, it was all about learning to take care of myself while she was using. Ultimately, it was a good thing, but I was disappointed. While attending Al-Anon meetings, I always believed with all my heart that my daughter would overcome her disease and become sober. I never expected that I would lose her forever to this terrible disease.

The October before she passed, I needed rotator cuff surgery and she offered to stay and take care of me. I was hesitant at first, but am so very grateful that she did. We became very close during that time, and, looking back, I see that time together as a huge gift. Two weeks before she succumbed to her disease, we celebrated her thirty-first birthday in Laguna Beach at what used to be The Beach House. These are treasured memories.

I was fifty-three years old when Mia died. She should have been burying me, not the other way around. The black abyss of grief is real. Most days I felt I was going to be sucked into that abyss. I felt like I was literally dying. I was having chest pain. I ended up in the hospital emergency room a few times during the first two years. According to Harvard Women's Health Watch, there actually is a true phenomenon called Takotsubo cardiomyopathy (broken-heart syndrome). It's named after an octopus trap. An ultrasound image can show abnormal movement in the wall of the left ventricle where the lower part balloons out during the contraction of the heart or systole. This bulging ventricle resembles a tako-tsubo, a pot used by Japanese fishermen to trap octopuses.

Interestingly, broken-heart syndrome occurs almost exclusively in women. Liz Szabo of USA Today writes about another condition that occurs exclusively in women. After giving birth, fetal cells remain in the mother's body and may provide stem cells to help the body repair damage. Mothers may be surprised to learn that they carry some of their children's cells for years or even decades after the end of a pregnancy. And while a baby photo can melt a mother's heart, the cells her child leaves behind in her blood may actually heal it, emerging research suggests.

The first year after losing Mia, I counted every day since she had been gone. I counted the days, hours, and minutes. I came to realize that the first year of grief was not the hardest; it was just the first of many hard years. Life was so hard. I became numb to anything else going on in the world, the news, music, television. I couldn't concentrate, and was unable to read a book, even though reading was something I had enjoyed my whole life. I could hardly get out of bed most days. If I brushed my teeth or took a shower I was really doing well. Holidays, and especially her birthday and Angelversary, were extremely difficult passages.

I surrounded myself with my extended family and tried to attend the traditional holiday family get-togethers, but it was trying. Family members yearned for me to be my old self, not understanding or accepting that I have become this new self. It was heartbreaking to see my siblings and their children continue on with their loving relationships. This made it difficult for me to be around people, even my own family. I didn't want pity; I didn't want to feel bitter, but the truth is that I am human. A human mother who has lost her child. Nobody wanted to talk about Mia, and if I did, someone would abruptly change the subject due to their own obvious discomfort. This caused me to feel shame. It felt like I was being forced to live without my beautiful blue-eyed girl and had to figure out how I was going to function in social settings. I learned to have a "Plan A" and a "Plan B." If Plan A was not working, then I moved to Plan B. My backup plan, Plan B, was an exit plan.

Every year I have what I call my "grief storm," which occurs from her birthday on February 23rd through March 8th, the anniversary of her death, or, as I like to call it, her "Angelversary." In the early years, my grief storm started at the beginning of the previous year's holidays and would end mid-March around the Spring Solstice. Over time it has shortened to this two-week period. After the eighth of March, a sense of renewal and new life fills me with relief. Each year the grief becomes softer, life without her more doable.

Her death has not only changed who I am, but how I react to the world. I have gained a stronger faith in God, a tender compassion for others who have experienced the loss of a child, and more empathy for others in general. These qualities have given me a new perspective—seeing life through the eyes of another. A favorite quote is: *"Be kind, for everyone is fighting a hard battle."* —Plato

Grief is different for everyone, for mothers and fathers, husbands and wives, siblings and grandparents. I watched my son and husband stuff their grief. Neither of them missed a day of work; neither wanted to talk about Megan after her death or would even look at a picture of her. Eventually, the grief exploded in both of them, expressed as anger. The anger has affected us personally, professionally, and spiritually.

The opposite was true for me, as I preferred to deal with the grief. I wanted to feel the feelings, to cry the tears, and then hopefully move on. I believe that tears can be healing. Just as the rain is beneficial to replenishing the earth, our tears can be beneficial in cleansing our souls of negative energy and sorrow after loss. I am a strong believer that it is healthy to grieve. It has helped move me through my healing in a timely manner. Sometimes the feelings of grief affect me daily, but sometimes I go weeks or months feeling good, able to laugh and enjoy the small pleasures in life. But when a memory, a song, or an anniversary hits, it hits hard, like a tidal wave. I have learned to ride the wave and become a strong swimmer. I know now that I will not drown.

Watching my son deal with the loss of his sister has been difficult. Dr. Christina Hibbert speaks of ten things she feels people need to know about sibling loss. "Because sibling loss is so misunderstood, messages of 'you should be over it by now' are common. There is no timeline. It takes time, lots of time. You don't get over it. You create your life and move on when you're ready. But you never forget your sibling, they will always be a part of you."

I have seriously struggled with guilt. Guilt is defined as: "an emotion that occurs when a person believes they have violated a moral standard; a cognitive or emotional experience that occurs when a person realizes or believes, accurately or not, that he or she has compromised his or her own standards of conduct or has violated a moral standard and bears significant responsibility for that violation. It is closely related to the concept of remorse, or anger and fear of rejection." I didn't know how to do anger, but boy was I good at feeling guilty. I have learned that nothing can change the past, however, and guilt is only useful if it provides motivation for positive change. It took me about five years to work through all my guilt associated with my daughter's death. I had to forgive myself and let go of the guilt. Forgiving ourselves can be harder than forgiving someone else.

After Mia's death, I started a Facebook page called Megan's Grace Foundation. My purpose has been to live my life with grace in her honor, and to educate others about the disease of addiction and mental health disorders. I hope to make a difference in the life of someone living with the disease of addiction. I'm passionate about emphasizing how kindness and education can help reduce the stigma of mental illness. Scholarships have been given in Mia's memory to needy women and children through the Megan's Grace Foundation.

Shortly after Mia passed, I was introduced to Origami Owl, a custom jewelry company, that could allow me to "tell my story" about my beautiful blue-eyed girl's life by making lockets. First, I made a living locket in her memory and wore it close to my heart. I now gift and sell these special pieces of jewelry to other family members, and to mothers who have lost a child, a loved one, or a fur baby. Through my website I have been making these lockets for nine years now.

A year after losing Mia, I decided to start a private lactation practice, instead of returning to lactation nursing in a hospital setting. I was fortunate to be invited to join a pediatric group where I was able to set up my own practice. By supporting mothers and families, helping them to sustain their infant through breastfeeding, I truly treat these mothers as if they were my own daughters.

One day at a time, I keep pushing past my vulnerabilities. My faith has become stronger as I have felt a desperate need to cling to a power greater than myself. I can place my sorrow, grief, anxiety, depression, and fears into His hands. This ability came from the tools gratefully gained while participating in the Al-Anon support group.

I have been forever changed since losing my daughter. I honestly cannot see myself ever being the person I was before Mia died. Friends and family may have trouble understanding that because they have not suffered the same unimaginable loss that I have. My advice on how to help a grieving parent is to reach out to them, because they are too numb to reach out to you. Also, recall memories of their child, send a card, say their child's name, pay it forward in their honor, light a candle in their memory, and be there just to listen. Not just in the first year or two, but every year. Our children will always be alive within our hearts and minds, no matter how much time has passed. We grieve because we love. How long does grief last? Hopefully, forever.

Thanks to a dear friend who started the Southern California support group, Solace for Hope, my "Sol" sisters remember each of our children's birthdays and memorial anniversary dates. This group is like family. There is no judgment; we are simply there for one another. We can share our deepest thoughts and emotions and no one silences or shames us. Together we know that our children are forever loved and never forgotten.

Another source of help for me was Umbrella Ministries, a faith-based grief group that offers opportunities to share your loss with others in a small group setting. They provide reading materials of support and encouragement, and hold annual women's retreats and conferences. I learned about this grief ministry through a fellow Al-Anon mother who had lost her son a year before Mia passed. A sister in Christ, she invited me to my first Umbrella Ministries meeting where, in a small intimate group, I met other beautiful women with whom I am still in touch to this day.

As long as I am breathing, I have hope as I move ahead through life without my firstborn. My compassion is infinite for other families who have lost a child. Over the years since Mia's death, family and friends have reached out to me, seeing me as a helpful resource for someone they know who has also lost their son or daughter. Some of these, once complete strangers, have later became dear friends.

Our loved one's spirits are strong and they surround us with their energy and love. Be open to their "God-winks" and their signs to comfort us. In the flutter of the osprey hawk outside my window, the snowy egret in the tall grass behind my home, the deer who greet me on my nature walks, and the rainbows that light up the sky after a summer's rain, I feel my Mia smiling down on me; I feel her laughter and her love.

Here are some of my favorite quotes that have helped my heart to heal:

> "When a child dies, there are two hearts that stop beating, the child's and the mother's. From the time of conception, they were "one." How can a mother's heart continue to beat when her child is no more? Only a mother can understand the depth of such love."
>
> —Author Unknown

> "I have found the paradox, that if you love until it hurts, there can be no more hurt, only more love."
>
> —Mother Teresa

> "The healing begins when we can start to feel more gratitude that our child came into our life than despair and outrage that our child died. The gratitude is what heals the despair."
>
> —Ram Dass

"Perhaps they are not star's, but rather openings in heaven where the love of our lost ones pours through and shines down upon us to let us know they are happy."

—ESKIMO PROVERB

"I would not exchange the laughter of my heart for the fortunes of the multitudes; nor would I be content with converting my tears. . .into calm. It is my fervent hope that my whole life on this earth will ever be tears and laughter."

—KAHLIL GIBRAN

Remember at the beginning of my story how I mentioned hearing the front door open while my husband and I slept? How we just assumed it was Mia coming in to sleep in the guest room as she often did, having no idea that she had passed away? I know for certain that I was not dreaming it when I heard the sound of the front door opening. Even though she did not *physically* come into the house, I believe her soul visited me that night to let me know she was okay, even better than okay, that she was now perfect. No more pain. No more addiction. No more anxiety. She was now in a state of perfection and at peace. I pray she wrapped her new soft angel wings around me, whispered in my ear that she loved me, and continued on to serve others in Paradise.

"For he shall give his angels charge over thee,
to keep thee in all thy ways."

—PSALM 91:11

CHAPTER 8

Maggie's Story

I am Maggie, and this is my story. I was born and raised in Northern California by parents of Mexican descent, and raised in a bilingual home within the beautiful Mexican culture. My parents worked hard to keep food on the table and provide for our ever-growing needs. We may not have had a lot, but we had what we needed.

As the third of four siblings, I was extremely shy and sensitive. My siblings would tease me, calling me a crybaby. I grew up hating being sensitive, and always felt different. However, I now believe being sensitive is an asset. I embrace being an empath, which has allowed me to love deeper and more unconditionally and show much-needed compassion toward others.

As a young child, I felt feelings of sadness inside and now recognize it was depression. In those days nobody really spoke about mental health. Whenever sad or upset, I dealt with these heavy feelings by napping as a way to escape. I learned to suffer in silence and became good at hiding my true feelings.

At age nineteen, I moved out of my childhood home and into my first studio apartment in downtown Palo Alto. It was exciting and I loved the feeling of independence. I worked for a large pharmaceutical company and met my husband-to-be in the workplace. We dated for many years before eventually marrying, then started our family right away. Over a period of ten years, we had four sons. I loved being a mother and was fortunate to be able to stay at home with my boys, raising them and volunteering wherever possible for many years. They were and are my life.

Mitch was my beautiful and healthy first-born son, born in April 1988. He was my joy and as a first-time mother I was in awe of this amazing little guy. He had a sweet, gentle disposition, was sensitive, and extremely shy. As early as six months old, I noticed he struggled to make eye contact with strangers. He was greatly attached to his dad and me, always needing to know where we were. I would even say he seemed uncomfortable in his own skin.

After a miscarriage, I then gave birth to my second son. Mitch, who was then age four, seemed to enjoy being a big brother, was a great mother's helper, and was proud of his baby brother. I would go on to suffer another miscarriage before having two more sons.

As a young boy, Mitch loved the game of hockey. Growing up, he played on several leagues and loved attending professional hockey games. We moved to Orange County when he seven. I can still remember him as the big kid on the block, teaching his siblings and other neighborhood children all about the game. Playing hockey, Mitch was in his element, but he struggled when it came to the classroom or other social settings. His shyness held him back in life. He never liked being the center of attention and seemed content to blend into the room. Mitch reminded me so much of myself. We had a special connection and were much alike as two sensitive souls.

In the summer of 2008, three of my sons and I went to visit my family in Lake Tahoe, but Mitch, age twenty, had decided to stay behind with his dad. By then he tended to isolate from family and most friends, and was even difficult to be around. We planned a week of fun-in-the-sun, rafting on the Truckee River with family. Two days before our return, my husband called with the shocking news that Mitch had been arrested. Mitch and his friend had been booked into an Orange County detention facility, charged with possession of heroin and drug paraphernalia, and a D.U.I. for being under the influence of a substance.

I cut our vacation short and announced to my boys we were leaving early the next day. On the drive home, I silently cried and prayed my boys would sleep most of the way, hoping they wouldn't see me crying. My goal was to get home as quickly as I could.

If given a do-over, I would have been more open with family and friends about Mitch and his struggles. We were overwhelmed, not understanding it was a disease, and that it can overtake every part of someone's life. We felt the shame and stigma that generally comes along with this disease. It became our little family secret. We remained silent, and silence can make us sick.

An attorney advised us to not post bail right away, in hopes that it would scare Mitch. We took the advice, thinking tough love would solve everything. We posted bail on the thirteenth day but only if Mitch agreed to enter a drug treatment program. Ultimately, he agreed to enter an outpatient program that consisted of three days a week of therapy, plus weekly family group therapy.

We felt progress was being made and we could finally begin talking about this crisis in our family. However, Mitch was not ready to admit he had a substance use disorder, and sadly, he was belligerent and disrespectful toward others at the weekly sessions, scoffing and smirking while others shared. I was ashamed by his behavior and didn't even recognize him. Another participant shared that he wished for a family as supportive as ours, and what he wouldn't give to have his parents attending the weekly sessions. The program director warned if Mitch couldn't admit he had a problem, he'd be discharged. And so he was, after only one month.

Within weeks he spiraled and began using again. Things began disappearing from our home. We hid things so he wouldn't use them as a means to purchase more drugs, although he always managed to find a way. We had so much to learn about this disease, but the problem is you think you have more time than you do.

The opposite of addiction is connection. A person who has a substance use disorder suffers greatly, and often alone and in silence. They retreat deeper into themselves and as their addiction worsens, their world around them becomes smaller. They stop caring about things that once mattered and lose hope and sight of dreams. They become desperate and must continue to use their drug of choice in order to stay well. This becomes all-consuming. Their every waking thought is about avoiding withdrawals.

Over the next two years, Mitchell spent his life trapped in the roller coaster ride of his disease. He tried his best as he managed to hold down jobs and even enrolled in auto mechanics courses, although no longer permitted to drive since he hadn't completed his D.U.I. class.

Over Memorial Day weekend, 2009, Mitch's addiction was ramping up; however, we did not understand the severity of it. My family was now living a different kind of existence within our own home, filled with anger, shame, and denial. Mitchell's dad began locking his controlled medications in a safe. One day he found hundreds of tiny broken pieces of pills and bits of plastic prescription bottles strewn all over the floor. The best way to describe this scene is that it looked as if a wild animal had ransacked the room. Mitch had pried through the small round hole in the back of the safe with a long screwdriver, then repeatedly stabbed at the prescription bottles until he was able to break them open, and then proceeded to shake the safe in order to get the loose pills to fall through the hole. This is just one example of the desperate lengths a person might resort to when suffering from a substance use disorder. Mitch was spiraling out of control and doing whatever necessary to avoid the horrible withdrawals from opiates.

As you can imagine, this was a shocking discovery, in which Mitch apologized and promised it wouldn't happen again. However, just two nights later his dad found him in my closet going through my purse. His dad told him that he had to leave immediately. So, on this rainy night he frantically packed his personal belongings, including things from his childhood years. Although heartbreaking, I agreed Mitch could no longer live there, and we abruptly tossed him out with no plan. Thankfully, his brothers weren't there to witness this painful scene.

My heart was breaking into a million pieces, and, to this day, the memory of that night remains painful. The next day I could just sense that Mitch was in trouble. Sure enough, he had been arrested. The police were called when Mitch was found tapping on the window of a stranger's home looking for shelter from the rain. What was happening to my son? His addictions had taken over his life and changed him into someone we no longer recognized.

Mitch's probation officer believed he was suffering from more than just an addiction issue, and so they wanted to assess him for a possible dual diagnosis. A dual diagnosis is the condition of suffering from a mental health disorder as well as a substance use disorder. He was removed from jail and placed into an Orange County Collaborative Court, called WIT, which stands for Whatever It Takes, a mental health court program. Mitch entered the program in August 2009 and was placed into a sober living home.

While engaged in this program, Mitch had a team of professionals supporting him, which consisted of a probation officer, case manager, therapist, and public defender. He was randomly drug tested and required to attend individual and group therapy sessions. We received positive feedback as he remained in compliance.

Right as we had arranged for a home visit, Mitch ended up breaking curfew and went missing. My heart sank as that feeling of dread returned. I sat in my car crying, knowing his dad and brothers would once again be disappointed. I checked online for who had been arrested overnight and was relieved to confirm his whereabouts, just to know he was alive. When a mother is relieved to learn her child is in jail, versus something much worse, it goes without saying how insane and abnormal her life has become.

Mitch had connected with a woman who was also in the WIT program, and together they broke curfew and violated their probation terms. There had been an altercation with another gentleman in which Mitch used his fist, which is considered a lethal weapon. Mitch had been charged with a violent felony. With this type of charge, it would reduce his chances of being eligible for drug court or other diversion programs. He now faced five years in state prison.

From September 2009 through June 2010, Mitch was remanded to additional incarceration time. After several court appearances, the judge took his dual diagnosis into consideration, and showed mercy on him. To my relief, he was given a reduced sentence and placed on a five-year formal probation. Mitch was caught in the justice system for one continuous year. But I loved him unconditionally, no matter what.

One day when visiting him at the detention center, I brought Mitch a check to sign. I met Mitch in a special area where a guard showed up and took the check from me and then gave it to him to sign. This guard had a problem with Mitch. The guard towered over Mitch as he sat there, signing the check, yelling and berating him. While the guard yelled at Mitch, I had a front row seat to my son being belittled and made to feel like he was a terrible waste of life. After the guard left, Mitch looked so humiliated. I fought back my tears, knowing Mitch's dignity had already been stripped, and me crying in front of him wasn't going to help.

Mitch acted like it was no big deal, just played it down. Fortunately, the guards inside were not all horrible to Mitch. He shared about a guard who had recognized him, and who turned out to be a young man who had known Mitch since grade school named Stewart. I thought about what that must have been like for Mitch, to be an inmate, and have a former classmate recognize you in that setting. But Mitch said Stewart was nice to him and whenever he saw Mitch he would go out of his way to be kind. I remember feeling like Mitch had an angel friend on the inside looking out for him, and I was grateful for that.

While incarcerated, Mitch's spirits were low and he felt quite hopeless. He didn't have many visitors and was sad about that. I tried my best to let him know he was loved and planted tiny seeds of hope for his future. During our visits we had deep conversations in which he shared some of his issues and feelings about his childhood. He always asked about his dad and brothers, but I often held back the good things in an attempt to avoid making him feel worse about his situation. Despite Mitch's struggles, he loved his brothers very much and was a fierce protector of them. This is something I hope his brothers will remember about him.

I continued to keep everything to myself, telling anyone who asked little white lies about Mitch and his life. It was easy to keep the big lie going, until one day when Mitch's nana announced she would be visiting. Mitch had made me promise to not tell her that he was in jail, since he was full of shame, but I knew she loved him unconditionally. As it turned out, her visits to him at the jail would be the last times she would see or speak to him.

I found a treatment program that was willing to accept him, and Mitch expressed his sincere desire to make needed changes. I remained in communication with the program about Mitch's release date and planned on driving him to the center on that day. On Monday, June 7th, 2010, Mitch was released around 1:00 am. After an entire year, my boy was finally home. I remember the exact spot in the kitchen where I insisted on getting my hugs.

Later that morning, Mitch called the program director and was told they weren't able to see him for several more days, at least until that Thursday. We'd never planned for him to be home with us for four days, but we weren't about to put him out into the streets. While at home he would be with me and wouldn't be allowed to leave the house to see or call friends.

During these four days at home, Mitch made three requests. He asked for a dental cleaning, since he wanted to enter the program with a fresh start, so I made him an appointment for early Thursday morning before we would leave for the treatment program. Next, he requested a cheeseburger and vanilla milkshake from Carl's Jr. He had craved this while in jail and wanted to enjoy it before he entered the program. I told him that I would try my best to make that happen, not knowing if we would have enough time. The third request was for a new pair of shoes. He wanted to begin this next phase of his life with new shoes rather than with the old ones that were full of holes. He ordered the shoes online and was excited they would arrive Friday.

Thursday Morning. We made our first stop Thursday morning for his dental cleaning, and thankfully he didn't have any cavities. Wish number one granted. Next, I dropped Mitch off at the treatment center for his four-hour assessment. My sincere hope was that he would surrender and embrace new ways of coping that didn't involve drugs. I was so naïve, not knowing that people with substance use disorders will struggle with this disease their entire life, and that there is no real cure.

After the assessment, I met privately with the program director. They confirmed Mitch had a dual-diagnosis and that they had the resources to help him, but would not be able to admit him into the program until the following morning. I couldn't believe that they were sending me home with him for one more night, and I begged them to keep him. They insisted he would be fine, that it was only one more night, and to bring him first thing in the morning. Although upset, I had to remain focused. That evening one of my sons had an event at school and I was rushed for time to get home. I knew I wouldn't have time to prepare dinner, so I insisted on getting Mitch something to eat. Unfortunately, there was no Carl's Jr. nearby but I saw an In-N-Out right before the freeway entrance. With the exception of it not being the exact burger place he wanted, I feel that I granted him wish number two.

Thursday evening. Once home I prepared for my other son's senior awards program. I could not have missed this awards night, since my son had worked hard and was due to receive several awards and scholarships. In fact, Mitch was planning to attend his brother's upcoming graduation and hoped to wear his new shoes. Mitch was uncomfortable in large crowds and asked if he could skip his brother's senior awards night. He promised not to contact anyone or go anywhere. As a show of trust, we left him behind. While away that evening I stepped out to call him. I was relieved when he seemed fine and reassured me that everything was okay.

When we returned, Mitch showed interest in his brother's event and was in a great mood. Later that evening, he walked into the kitchen for a glass of water. I saw him nodding off while standing up holding his glass and questioned him. He became annoyed with me, saying he was tired and to stop bothering him. Later I noticed him nodding off while sitting at the computer. I asked what was wrong, which further agitated him. I became angry, telling him how disappointed I was that he would use again knowing he was entering treatment in the morning.

I didn't understand his struggle. I knew so little about substance use disorders, and could not comprehend this was a critical situation, that Mitch, after a lengthy period of sobriety, now had no tolerance to drugs. Since Mitch wasn't honest with me that night, I had no idea how to help him. We agreed he would just sleep it off—a common, yet often fatal assumption. I couldn't have known it but this would be my last conversation with my son.

Friday morning. My husband was up getting ready for work while everyone slept. I awoke a little before 6:00 am and heard the television on in the guest room. I looked for the T.V. remote, and noticed it was in Mitch's hand. As I reached for the remote I immediately sensed something was terribly wrong. I called out Mitch's name and shook him lightly. This is when shock and the panic took over. When I failed to get a response, I began to pace as denial crept in. I ran upstairs to get my husband and together we tried to awaken him. We called 911 and attempted to begin C.P.R., but we were too late. Our home began to fill with first responders: paramedics, police, firefighters, trauma intervention volunteers, and the dreaded coroner.

We made the decision to wake up the boys since we didn't want to frighten or shock them if they should happen to wake up and make this discovery on their own. We gathered them in one room and broke the news. The wailing sounds that came from them were not human-like. At the time, Mitch's brothers were only twelve, fifteen, and eighteen years old. My heart broke in a million pieces that morning, June 11th, 2010.

Mitch had reached out on social media while we were at his brother's school event the night before. He had no money but had agreed to exchange his legitimately prescribed medications for black tar heroin. The exchange occurred in our front yard, right under our noses. This explains the nodding out, something referred to as the heroin nod. Once we were upstairs, he used the remaining heroin. His body had no tolerance and he'd used too much, too fast. About two hours after I found him, there was a knock at the door. Mitch's shoes arrived, thus almost granting his third wish. When he had ordered the shoes just two days before, who would have thought that by the time they arrived he would no longer be alive on this earth.

The fallout. After the loss of a child, you think about all the things you wish you had said or done. Hindsight is always 20/20, but if I'd had the knowledge back then that I have today, I could have helped my son so much more. Of course, it's a waste of time to stay stuck in these thoughts, as I will never have the answers to any of these questions. However, major mistakes were made. Telling my story needs to include these mistakes, as well as the lessons that were learned, if for nothing more than to spare another family from the same devastating loss.

Yes, there were things I didn't know about substance use disorders, and that's on me. Maybe I should have educated myself better. However, there were others who *did* know more and they neglected to inform me. The day before Mitch passed, I met with the program director, where he instructed us to return the next day. However, I believe I could have been sent home much better prepared. No one mentioned "The Last Hurrah," when someone wants to use drugs for the last time before entering treatment. I should also have been informed about the warning signs of an overdose. Instead, I was sent home with no instruction, no defense.

A week after my son passed, when I finally had a tiny semblance of strength in my voice, I asked why they hadn't warned me about what to possibly expect. The program representative just assigned the blame to me, stating that I should have known about The Last Hurrah. Their words cut deep, like they were putting all blame on me. I told him in the future not to assume families were informed and that they should take a few moments to educate them. These unfortunate assumptions directly contributed to Mitch's death.

I've made it part of Mitchell's mission to inform other families so the same tragic mistakes are not made. The death of my son inspired me to become a certified Narcan trainer, so I, and others, can save lives. I can't bear the thought of another parent being unprepared and defenseless like I was. Saving lives helps me make a little sense out of my son's death, so I know his life has value and purpose—that perhaps this was to be his purpose in life.

Since losing Mitch my life has forever changed. To lose a child is devastating. There really are no words to describe this loss. When a parent loses a child, they also lose a big part of themselves. Our futures now look different without our loved ones in it. A parent should not ever outlive a child.

The first two years of my grief journey, I truly didn't care if I lived. But because I know Mitch wouldn't want me to give up, or spend my life blaming myself, I wake up every day making a conscious choice to live. At times it feels like you are not deserving of anything good or beautiful in your life. In the early years you might catch yourself smiling or laughing, and then feel guilty for it. People tell you that it wasn't your fault, that there's nothing you could have done. However, nothing anyone says can ever fix or resolve our grief.

Well-meaning family and friends tell you that you have other children to be grateful for. It's not that I am not grateful for my other children, but they are not interchangeable spare parts; one can't take the place of another. In fact, when a grieving mother has surviving children, she also spends her days worrying about how they are dealing, or not dealing, with their own grief.

Losing a loved one to a substance disorder and mental health challenges is complicated. Many families remain silent, due to shame or stigma, which further complicates grief. For an impacted family, life is never the same. I know I could let it destroy my life or I could take this deeply profound loss and use it to help others going through similar experiences. I use my pain and purpose to give others hope, showing them that it is possible to survive the death of a child.

So, in 2012 I co-launched a support community called Solace For Hope (formerly known as Solace Orange County). The meetings provide a safe place for families who've lost a loved one to a substance use disorder or mental health challenge, and families who currently struggle with a loved one's substance use disorder, to share openly and without judgment. The meetings have now expanded to include people from the recovery community, which includes treatment programs, local colleges, and participants from the Orange County Drug Court Program. This is the club no one wants to belong to, yet ironically, once you're in this club it would be difficult to survive without the other members. Together we grieving parents remember our loved ones, their birthdays, memorial dates, and all the other days in between. We say their names and are not afraid to talk about them. We do not impose upon each other the unfair expectations for how long the grief process takes. Grief takes as long as grief takes.

In addition to the meetings, we created a Solace For Hope Meditation Garden, in the city of Tustin, CA. This is a sacred, peaceful space to honor our lost loved ones, which includes a memorial rock garden.

To learn more about Solace For Hope,
visit: www.solaceforhope.org

Solace For Hope recently partnered with Gibson Gives and the TEMPO program, Training and Empowering Musicians to Prevent Overdose. Tempo is a new program to help save musicians' lives in response to continuing opioid overdoses. This program is designed to empower participating nonprofits to provide life-saving Narcan training to help prevent opioid overdoses.

Do not be afraid to speak my son's name
If it brings tears to my eyes
it's not because you reminded me that he's gone
For this I could never forget
It's because you remembered him, his life, and honored his memory
Simply by saying his name.

Mitchell Craig Fleitman
4/15/88 ~ 6/11/2010
Forever Age 22

CHAPTER 9

Sandy's Story

*H*i, I am Sandy. I was born and raised in Orange County, California with wonderful parents and three siblings. I chose dental hygiene for my career and attended Cerritos College and U.C.L.A. for my education. My husband, Gary, and I have been married since August 1989. We live in Laguna Niguel, California and have three children: Garrett (25), Kendall (22), and Christian (forever 14-1/2). Currently, I stay busy working as a dental hygienist, traveling, enjoying family game nights, watching Angels baseball games, working out, and running our non-profit organization, Gold Rush Cure Foundation, where I am the co-founder and president.

Up until Christian's cancer diagnosis on May 7, 2006, we were your typical family, filling our weekends with our kid's soccer, baseball, and softball games. We loved every minute of our busy schedule. Until that fateful day, our oldest child, Christian, was a typical twelve-year-old boy. He filled his spare time with video games, soccer, computers, drawing funny cartoons, and just having fun. Christian had been exceptionally healthy his entire life, and excelled in school with straight As and near-perfect attendance.

Initially, some bruises on Christian's body caught my attention, but I thought they may have been related to a virus. A week later, on his thirteenth birthday, he now had over thirty large new bruises on his body, a horrific sight, and was also feeling tired and feverish. I called the doctor and requested a full blood panel. Not long after, we got the call that further testing would be required at Children's Hospital Orange County (C.H.O.C.). A bone marrow aspirate was done the next morning, which revealed that Christian had acute lymphoblastic leukemia (A.L.L.). No parent is prepared to hear, "Your child has cancer."

My heart just broke when we received the devastating news, and there were lots of tears. Christian was very scared and just wanted to go home. Instead, intense testing and treatment began the very next day. Two tubes were surgically inserted into his chest so the blood draws, chemo, and transfusions would be less painful. The chemo began with a vengeance. Three weeks later, when Christian still wasn't in remission, his oncologist delivered devastating news: the cytogenetic test results showed that Christian had a very rare chromosomal abnormality (occurring in fewer than one percent of all leukemia patients) called hypo-diploid acute lymphoblastic leukemia. This diagnosis put Christian in the highest risk group. He would require a bone marrow transplant (B.M.T.), which is extremely aggressive treatment.

After researching the best possible place for Christian's B.M.T., we decided that the Fred Hutchinson Cancer Research Center/Seattle Cancer Care Alliance offered the most promise. In preparation for the B.M.T., Christian would need to undergo extremely strong chemotherapy and total body irradiation. The goal was to kill everything in the bone marrow to clear the way for the B.M.T. The process was incredibly brutal but was our only hope.

A week later we received great news: Christian's younger brother, Garrett, and sister, Kendall, were both bone marrow matches. Thank you, Lord! Both kids were hoping to be chosen to be Christian's donor because they so wanted to help him get well. The doctors decided on Garrett because he was bigger and of the same gender.

Kendall, Garrett, and I flew to Seattle on July 24th (Garrett's 11th Birthday) on a private plane. A dear friend organized this flight, since it wasn't safe for Christian to fly on a commercial airline, due to his compromised immune system. I was concerned that this wouldn't be a very special birthday for Garrett, but the Lord worked that out too. In the private plane terminal at Orange County Airport, Garrett ran into two Major League Baseball players, David Eckstein (former Angel) and Jim Edmonds. Garrett, who is a huge baseball fan and played baseball for years, recognized the guys and was very excited to meet them. Wearing his Angels Baseball hat as usual, got to talk to David and take a photo with him. That photo is still so very special to him. While we were in flight to Seattle, Gary drove my car to meet us there so I would have transportation.

Our family checked into the Seattle Ronald McDonald House, which became our home away from home. They were wonderful and did all they could to help us and the other families who were also in our shoes. We fell into a very busy schedule of clinic and doctor appointments. As a family, we also made a huge effort to have some fun, too.

The Ronald McDonald House (R.M.H.) ended up being such a blessing to us. I would leave the hospital early each morning so I could return back again before Christian woke up. After a quick run for stress relief, I headed to the R.M.H. to take a shower, and to make batches of my famous chocolate chip cookies for the nurses and doctors. I would return to the hospital each day with warm cookies for everyone, and they loved them. It was my little love language, my way of expressing gratitude for the incredible care the doctors and nurses provided for Christian and many other children battling cancer.

Christian's B.M.T. day was referred to as "Christian's second birthday." Garrett had his surgery in the morning to remove over 750 cc of bone marrow. He was so nervous about the surgery, but also excited that he could help his big brother. Our hope was that Garrett's cells would take over, killing any remaining cancer cells in Christian's blood. We felt blessed to have Dr. Carpenter perform Garrett's bone marrow harvest because we had developed so much confidence in him during Christian's treatment.

As we waited for the transplant to kick in, Garrett and Christian often had fun playing video games with Taylor Carol, a fellow patient who became their good friend and Christian's B.M.T. partner. Taylor and his family were there to help us through difficult challenges when our family couldn't be there together, and we became close friends. Another patient the kids loved seeing was Bailey Rocha, along with her siblings. We became close to the Rocha family, too. The close friendships that are formed during this journey are the beautiful silver linings.

My mom, Ginni, stayed at our house in Orange County to be there for Garrett and Kendall when they returned home, as well as to care for our puppies. She kept the kids busy with luncheon dates with various family and friends. Kendall's eighth birthday was September 1st and, being in Seattle still, I missed it. I also missed their first day of school that following week. I was sad and torn because Garrett and Kendall needed me, too, and I couldn't be there for them, but I was very thankful I could be in Seattle for Christian.

We tackled Christian's schoolwork daily. Thankfully, he was an awesome student, which made up for me not being an awesome teacher. I formed a new respect for teachers during this time. One day, we received a wonderful phone call from our doctor; the test showed Christian's blood was clear of cancer cells now and Garrett's cells were kicking butt. Thank you, God! After being in the hospital for fifty-two of the last sixty-four days, it was finally time to go home. Christian and I had been in Seattle for nearly five months. We were so excited to go home to California, once his central line was surgically removed. Even though Christmas was only a couple of weeks away, with no presents bought, no decorations up, it really didn't matter. All that mattered to us was we would be home and together as a family.

We made it home shortly before Christmas, put up a tree loaded with fun, homemade ornaments, and enjoyed our holiday. A few weeks after the New Year, Mr. Grim, the principal at Stoneybrooke Junior High, called and told me they would love for Christian to participate in the graduation ceremony with his class. That was so cool, and Christian got a big smile on his face when I told him. It was so great that he was able to graduate with the kids he had gone to school with since kindergarten.

Just one month later, I noticed some bruising and red spots on Christian's skin, called petechiae, and my stomach immediately felt sick. I knew it was a sign of low platelets, which was a sign of relapse. We had a clinic appointment that day, so I let the oncologist know what I'd found and begged her to tell me that he hadn't relapsed. They drew labs and the test showed 78% cancer cells in Christian's bone marrow. We were all devastated! He was transported by ambulance to Children's Hospital Los Angeles (C.H.L.A.). Gary and I were now faced with making choices that were literally life or death decisions for our child.

After surgery to insert a new central line, they started a stronger chemo that produced an anaphylactic reaction in addition to horrific side effects. A few weeks later, labs showed that Christian was finally in remission, and we headed back to Seattle for his second B.M.T. The Chaplin came and "blessed" the cells and prayed for Christian. Several of the wonderful nurses came in and sang "Happy Transplant Day To You." Although Kendall wanted to be Christian's donor this time, the doctors opted for a non-related donor. This anonymous, selfless person sent a beautiful card to Christian a few weeks later through the hospital.

Because Christian was still in Seattle recovering from the second B.M.T., he, sadly, missed his eighth grade graduation. However, while Christian was still at C.H.L.A., Mr. Grim was kind enough to come to the hospital and hand-deliver Christian's diploma. Mr. Grim played the video of this special moment at the graduation ceremony, and everyone gave Christian a standing ovation. It was deeply touching.

We got to leave the hospital for a few hours on a pass for the July 4th holiday. Christian really wanted to see some fireworks this year because he had been in the hospital the last Fourth of July. Gary found a park that was hosting fireworks, so we found a secluded place and enjoyed the show. Anything to bring a smile to Christian's face.

The months passed. Gary, Garrett, and Kendall continued to fly up to visit Christian and me every other week. We really looked forward to these weekends when our family could be together. Christian also looked forward to taking his Make-A-Wish (M.A.W.) trip at some point when he was healthy. My best friend, Kelli, worked at M.A.W. Los Angeles and made Christian an amazing notebook with several different destinations to pick from, starting from A-Z. He was so excited to go but, sadly, was never well enough to take his Wish trip.

About a month later, we received the devastating news that Christian's latest tests showed he had relapsed again. Telling Christian this news was heartbreaking and he was so sad. Gratefully, two weeks later, and after more chemo infusions, his tests showed he was once again back in remission. We were still praying and hopeful that the "donor cells" were "searching and destroying" every last cancer cell because Christian's cancer was so aggressive and sneaky. Sadly, he had nearly a one hundred percent chance of relapsing again.

Gary was with me in Seattle for my birthday on September 30th. We had a great talk with Christian. After a painful and sad day, we asked him to walk a little with us and, although he was extremely sick and weak, he did. What a trooper! We told him how proud of him we are, how happy we are that he is our son, how God is using him in such a huge way, and how much we love him. He said, "Mom, I want to get out of the hospital so I can be out for your birthday." He was always thinking of others. I told him that my birthday didn't matter and that we'd celebrate both our birthdays when we got back to California.

A few weeks later, Christian became extremely sick. His graft-versus-host disease (G.V.H.D.) was worsening. Some G.V.H.D. is good because graft-versus-leukemia is helpful where the donor cells go after the cancer cells that are trying to come back. But his G.V.H.D. levels being so high indicated that his liver was not functioning well.

Some weeks later, Christian almost died. He was placed on N.P.O. (no food) because his gut was still sloughing the lining damaged by the G.V.H.D., which was causing hemorrhaging. We were now at day thirty-six in the hospital for this stay, and my poor son felt so isolated and sick. Christian was sad he would spend yet another Halloween in the hospital.

When Thanksgiving week arrived, we decided to start mentioning the things we were thankful for. As a special treat, a group at the R.M.H., called "The Basket Brigade," made up mainly of teens, came by and dropped off everything we would need for a Thanksgiving feast. Although very thankful that our family was together, it was still a hard day because Christian was so very sick and hemorrhaging even more. It is brutal watching your child endure such suffering! As his mother, I would have given anything to take his suffering from him.

My mom flew up to Seattle to join us for Thanksgiving, and together we surprised Kendall by taking her to get her ears pierced. This had been a wish of hers for a while. Kendall was so surprised and happy. It was a fun "girl's day" out with lunch, ear piercing, and shopping. Days like these were so important for maintaining our sanity.

Making Lemonade out of Lemons — Question: What do you do when you have a day that goes really bad (Thanksgiving)? Answer: You run out to Target for Christmas decorations to decorate Christian's hospital room. And decorate we did! Kendall and I drew Christmas scenes on the windows of his room, we hung lights all over, and we even decorated a small fiber optic tree with ornaments. With the Christmas decorations up and the "Smiling Faces Walls." hundreds of happy photos people sent per our request that now covered all his walls. Christian's hospital room now looked beautiful and festive.

As Christmas drew near, Christian, sadly, grew weaker. While we received the good news that Christian was cancer-free, the bad news was that the G.V.H.D. was overtaking his liver and body. Two days before Christmas, Gary and I were given the heartbreaking news that Christian might not survive much longer. This news compelled us to sit down with Garrett and Kendall, suggesting it was time to say the things they wanted their brother to know, in case he didn't pull through.

Although Christian was very ill, he was still fighting to stay with us. I already knew he was the fiercest warrior I had ever seen, but I truly could not comprehend how he withstood the hemorrhaging and all his terrible suffering. Even though some people expressed the concern that Christian be allowed to "go peacefully," his words and actions told us that leaving was not what he wanted. As long as Christian wanted to keep up the fight, we would continue to fight with him and for him.

Christmas Day brought horrible news; Christian coded on Christmas morning before being resuscitated. Gary and I were told our beautiful son would die soon, and so we signed the Do Not Resuscitate document on Christmas Day. His pain medicine had been increased several times that day, so he was in and out of sleep. When talking to the doctors, they all felt his G.V.H.D. was too far advanced, there was too much damage done to his body and vital organs, and his body was just too weak to pull through this. We wouldn't prolong things just to keep him with us if he was in pain. His body would tell us when the time had come. We had battled this journey alongside Christian since day one. For those of you who have had to make that decision for your child, our aching hearts are right there with you.

The day after Christmas, it was apparent that the time was near. The following day, the doctors took Christian off of hydration, and we were told it would only be a matter of hours before he'd be gone. Christian was still fighting to stay alive, just as hard as he'd fought the cancer. His heart is *so* big and strong, both literally and figuratively, that, although most of his organs had shut down, his heart and lungs were still functioning. Our family members took turns lying next to him while he slept until he took his final breath.

After a twenty-month battle, which included over sixteen months in the hospital, countless chemo treatments and transfusions, total body irradiation, three cancer relapses, over fifty bone marrow aspirates and lumbar punctures, numerous surgeries and procedures, months of isolation, G.V.H.D., and liver failure, Christian earned his angel wings on December 29, 2007 at 10:42 pm while in the arms of his family. We are proud beyond words when we think about the fight he put up, the courage he showed, and the faith he maintained.

Our hearts were absolutely broken but we knew he was now pain-free in heaven. These are the verses we posted when Christian earned his angel wings:

> I have fought the good fight, I have finished the race, I have kept the faith. There is in store for me the crown of righteousness, which the Lord, the righteous Judge, will award to me on that day.
>
> —2 TIMOTHY 4:7-8

> His master replied, "Well done, good and faithful servant!"
>
> —MATTHEW 25:21

A couple of hours after Christian passed, I opened the door to his room to find several of his special "primary" nurses had come, in addition to the Chaplain, my friend, and two of Christian's doctors. Even at that late hour, they'd come to support our family and to pay their respects to Christian. These special nurses helped us clip some locks of Christian's hair to save, in addition to many other priceless memories. In addition, some of these nurses, and my dear friend Colleen from Seattle, even flew to California to attend Christian's "Celebration of Life" service. I will carry these beautiful memories with me forever. Christian's doctors and nurses will hold a special place in my heart always and I will never forget the love and compassion they gave Christian, especially Drs. Carpenter, Delaney, Manley, Andrews, and nurses Brooke, Shauna, Tracie, Amber, and Suzanne. They are truly angels on earth.

After Christian died, so many details had to be quickly taken care of. Thank God for our dear friends. Gina took care of the process to get Christian flown back to California. Our friends Lynn and Chris ended up coming to our aid, too, not only when Christian died, but when we had to pack up our belongings and send them home. They even drove my car back to California so we could fly home to start making Christian's "Celebration of Life" arrangements. Our friend Jo kindly arranged for the flight, and many loving friends helped us plan the service once we arrived back home. It truly did "take a village" to take on such an undertaking, and we were blessed with an incredible and loving village.

I have experienced the loss of my dad and other people I loved very much, and that was heartbreaking, but *nothing* compares to losing your child. Your children are literally a part of you, and watching them grow and thrive brings so much joy to a mom and dad. A piece of yourself goes with your child when they pass away.

I think a mother takes on her other kids' grief and suffering, too. I definitely did that with Garrett and Kendall, which amplified my own grief. I still worry about the impact this journey has had on them. Thankfully, Gary and I are blessed with a solid marriage that remains strong. I have managed my grief through my strong faith, loving family support, therapy, and by reminding myself that, while I ache for where Christian isn't (with us), I am happy for him for where he is (Heaven). I know his suffering is gone. Gary and I didn't waste time asking the futile question: "Why me?" Instead we asked, "What now?" There was no way we would let this journey and Christian's death be in vain. We prayed for direction and God inspired a passion for advocacy work and support for other childhood cancer families on our hearts.

Two years after Christian passed away, Gary and I started Gold Rush Cure Foundation. Christian Gordon Barker (5/6/1993 - 12/29/2007) became the inspiration for Gold Rush Cure Foundation (G.R.C.F.), which is a 501c3 non-profit organization that supports children battling cancer through our Pot-of-Gold gifting program, while also advocating on a legislative level for new research and less toxic cures. I was asked to go to Washington, D.C. to be a childhood cancer advocate just three months after Christian died. After experiencing Christian's heartbreaking cancer journey firsthand, and seeing how little is being done to find cures for this disease, a fire was ignited inside me to become a voice for these amazing children and families.

Since Christian passed thirteen years ago, I have made almost thirty trips to Washington, D.C. I have been invited to speak at the World Stem Cell Summit, Regenerative Medicine conferences, and have helped mentor and educate other advocates and families who are faced with a childhood cancer diagnosis. G.R.C.F. is now represented in one hundred children's hospitals nationwide and we have delivered over seven hundred Pots-of-Gold gifts to families. A "Pot-of-Gold" is a customized $500 gift for children battling cancer, and their siblings, too, because they are just as important and loved as the child cancer hero.

It is surreal to see how our foundation has grown. A large part of this is due to wonderful, dedicated board members who have a heart for this cause and for the amazing children and families we serve. The work we are doing by no means negates the pain of losing Christian, but we know he is happy to see that our efforts are delivering hope to so many children battling cancer, and to their families. I also think this work helps us heal.

They say our true colors are revealed when we face adversity. Christian showed us his true colors through his incredible courage, determination, respect, compassion for others, and faithfulness in God. I will always thank God for letting me be the mom of three special children, even though I had to give one back to Him. We are truly blessed to see how Christian's life and legacy have impacted so many people through the work G.R.C.F. does today. We will continue this work until our vision—"Inspiring hope, delivering joy, and pursuing a cure until no child has cancer"—is realized!

Gold Rush Cure Foundation: www.goldrushcure.org

CHAPTER 10
Karon's Story

*H*i, my name is Karon, and this is my story.

I had what most people would refer to as a "normal" childhood, with the exception that we moved around quite a bit during my formative years: South Dakota, Arizona, then back to South Dakota, and finally, while still in high school, we landed in Southern California, just a short walk from the beach. My mom was raised Mennonite and she and dad met in a small Christian boarding school in South Dakota. They taught and raised me to love Jesus. At just eighteen years of age, I married my high school sweetheart, Jeff, and yes, we are still in love after forty years of marriage. I attended community college and U.C.L.A. a couple of years after we were married and became a registered dental hygienist. We waited ten years before we had children, and eventually had three sons: Thomas, Jeffrey (J.V.), and Bryce.

Our life was very busy but satisfying. I must admit, looking back, we were not perfect parents, but we were good parents who loved our children. We took a great deal of pride in being very involved in our son's lives, volunteering in schools, coaching, teaching Sunday school, and helping out in kid's youth groups. My husband is a hard-working man, and this allowed me to work part-time and be at home with our sons more. My parents provided all of our childcare when I worked, which was an incredible blessing.

Thomas and Bryce have beautiful stories with struggles of their own, but I was asked to share the story of our beautiful, brown-eyed middle boy, J.V. He was such an easy child to love! In fact, J.V. was very well liked by everyone. Even his delivery into this world was easier than the other two boys. We raised our family in San Clemente, CA, where we have lifelong friends and a wonderful church family. Our boys experienced an idyllic childhood growing up in a beautiful beach town where so many families know and care about each other.

In grade school, J.V. was an excellent student and loved by his teachers. In his early years the children's director at church offered him a scholarship to camp because he was such a good influence on others. He was very popular in school, girls calling *all* the time. He was a very skilled body boarder, becoming a state champ in middle school and even placing second in nationals. After the age of thirteen or so, though, he never competed again, although he remained an avid waterman the rest of his life. J.V. was incredibly kind. He knew the homeless in town by name and shared whatever he had with them.

He had a pretty special peer group as well. I taxied those young men all over town and we often had sleepovers with six to ten boys because it was too hard to leave anyone out. Somewhere along the way, however, things began to change. J.V. was the "cool" kid and to keep up that image it seemed he had to be edgier and edgier as time went on. Alcohol and substance abuse crept in. Friends changed. We could see these disturbing changes happening, yet felt powerless to stop them.

After high school he attempted to attend community college, but his heart was not in it. He rarely spent time at home anymore. When we did see J.V., he looked unhealthy and unhappy. At some point along the way, hope crept in for a short time, as he seemed to make a change for the better. In fact, eventually J.V. moved back home, got a full-time job, and seemed to be turning the corner.

Not long after, though, the unthinkable happened. The phone call that no parent ever wants to answer came in the middle of the night. Earlier that evening we had enjoyed a family dinner and then a big clothes-shopping spree with all three sons so they could spend their Christmas money. The phone call was from his distraught girlfriend of several years. She called to inform us that, unbelievably, J.V. had jumped off a freeway bridge, was struck by a truck, and had died in her arms while lying in the middle of the freeway. The toxicology report showed evidence of drugs in his system.

That horrific night changed everything for Jeff and me. How do you survive such a thing? Losing a child! Losing a child to *suicide*. For us, we were able to survive by hanging on to each other, desperately clinging to Jesus and the incredible support offered by friends, family, and extended church family. Our kids even jokingly said, "You need support for your support!" People were so very generous we couldn't even store all the food brought to us. Finally, after three months of delicious meal support, we could accept no more. We truly felt and appreciated the prayers of so many. It was very hard to get out of bed, yet we did, day after day. We had two other sons who needed us, and we had a mortgage. We had to act alive until we could *feel* alive again.

I have had many female mentors throughout my life. One such mentor, a patient and very godly woman, suggested I read *One Thousand Gifts* by Ann Voskamp and *The Great Lie* by Martha Kilpatrick. God used *The Great Lie* to help me keep my faith. What really resonated with me in that book was the idea that either God is sovereign and good, or he is not. Another book that was helpful when confronting my doubts was *The Shack* by William P. Young. I would recommend these books to any mother whose world has been shaken by the loss of a child.

I faithfully wrote in my journal about three things I was thankful for everyday for the first two years after losing J.V. God used those exercises of gratefulness to keep me from sinking into deep depression. In addition to journaling, music also provided relief from the effects of grief. I assembled some playlists that helped to soothe me or to lift me up.

I was also given a book of poetry by a dear friend entitled *To Bless the Space Between Us,* by John O'Donohue. I found this quote to be important for suicide loss survivors: "May the angel of wisdom enter this ruin of absence and guide your minds to receive this bitter chalice so that you do not damage yourselves by attending only at the hungry altar of regret and anger and guilt."

Just a word of caution here for other mothers who have lost a child to suicide. There are so many "what-ifs" that follow a suicide death. We blame ourselves; we blame others. It is normal to spend some time here, but don't be consumed with the what-ifs. What-ifs just paralyze us, and keep us from moving forward. The pastor at our son's memorial called suicide an accident of the mind. I think that is a very good description. I also like the glass of water analogy. One drop doesn't make the glass overflow. It's an accumulation of moments (drops) in their lives.

That first year was rough, but I was completely unprepared for the second year, which was incredibly difficult. Jeff and I grieved very differently, and we had to accept that. Cleaning was my diversion. I organized our house from top to bottom, and then I moved on to cleaning my parent's cabin. I found myself doing things I had always feared . . . like climbing under the cabin in a Tyvek suit and respirator and cleaning out all of the rat-infested insulation.

I was on a mission to *not* feel. I was angry, angry at God. After all, He hadn't saved my boy. It was a dark time. I'm reminded of a C.S. Lewis quote from *A Grief Observed*: "Not that I am in much danger of ceasing to believe (I think) in God, the real danger is of coming to believe such dreadful things about Him." I came to resent the logic surrounding the idea that God "allows" or "causes" these events in my life. It all became a matter of semantics. I began wrestling with God. I had wrestled with him years before after losing my brother to suicide. I tried to be respectful; He is Almighty God after all. I don't have all the answers and I don't understand God or why I lost J.V. Quite frankly, if I am able to understand God, then he's not big enough.

There is free will in this life, mine, of course, as well as others around me, and it bears enormous consequences. I choose not to believe the lie that God is not good. "God's will is good because God is good, not because I like it" —Martha Kilpatrick, *The Great Lie.*

After a good amount of time had passed, I was invited to a "Grieving Mommas" group. It was there that I discovered a group of other women who were all going through the same type of pain. It was suggested that I try journaling, but I'm not a writer, and, other than my daily gratitude list, I didn't really "do" journaling. Then one Sunday afternoon, I found myself wanting to get out of the house and I ended up at the very same venue as my first date with Jeff nearly

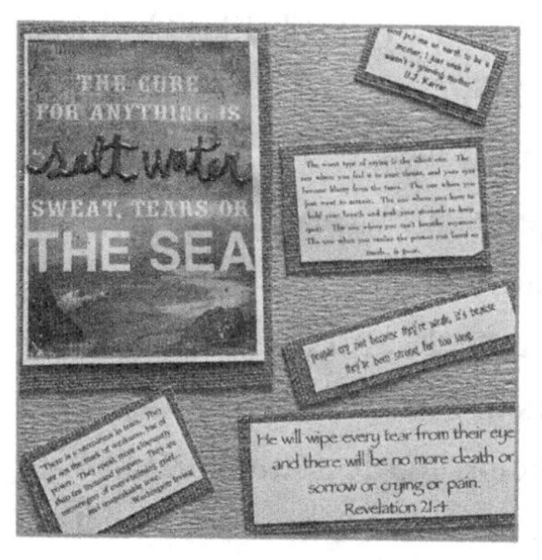

thirty years before—the Sawdust Festival, an annual art show held in Laguna Beach, CA. While walking through the artists' booths, I came across an artist doing collages with poignant little sayings. I thought to myself, "Hey, I can do that."

I started making artistic collages with grief quotes that I had found from all different sources, and it turned out to be very cathartic. I even wrote a couple of my own quotes. Eventually, I produced a few copies of my "grief journal," which I'd filled with these colorful and therapeutic collages, through Shutterfly, and have since sent these books to others going through grief of their own. Helping others with their grief process has helped alleviate my own.

Losing a child changes your perspective. It seems that now nothing is too difficult anymore—even when it feels like the worst of life is being thrown at us. In reality, the rest of our life is pretty darn good! I guess what I mean to say is, you don't take yourself and problems so seriously after something like this. We are Christians and this world isn't our home. We are here to glorify God and we pray we do that by how we actually live our lives; words alone cannot do that.

It is now a well-known fact that drug-related deaths and drug-related suicides have increased dramatically in the past decade. Overdoses and suicides are still surrounded by a powerfully negative stigma in our society. Jeff and I have not started any foundations or been speakers or anything big like that. Instead, it felt like God just wanted us to stand after what we'd been through. "Just survive," I kept telling myself—but not just survive, survive *well.*

We now realize that this sort of tragedy can happen to any good, loving family. It happens all the time, sadly. It seems we always hear that trauma causes bad choices. Looking back, and maybe I'm blind here, but I don't see any horrible traumas in our son's life. Choices are made that can cause trauma. Jeffrey Vincent made some bad choices and those choices had tragic consequences. As time goes by, you start to question everything you did as a mother in raising your kids. I often question how much I enabled them in certain areas that may have contributed to bad behavior and bad habits. As a mother, you can't help but wonder.

Unfortunately, it didn't take others long to point this out. "After all," I kept telling myself, "they are all looking for reasons as to how this could happen as well." The frustrating part of this inference, however, was the fact that we didn't feel we had done any more for our children than anyone else we knew. In fact, I was reminded, soon after, of the old saying: "When you help your children and they make 'wise' choices, you are 'empowering' them; when they make 'bad' choices, you are 'enabling' them."

This journey has been incredibly painful, but also very beautiful. I believe in a BIG God and I firmly believe that I will see my beautiful J.V. again.

CHAPTER 11

Suzanne's Story

*M*y name is Suzanne. I am a fifty-three-year-old wife of twenty-three years to my greatest love, and the mother of three amazing children, two living on this earth and one in heaven. I'm also a grandmother (Nani) to one grandson. I was born and raised in Southern California, where I continue to reside. This is my story about love and loss, heartbreak and acceptance.

I learned I was pregnant with Christopher when I was just twenty-two years old. I married my first husband, Christopher's father, that same year. I then had my second son the following year, so I was busy and so very young! My boys were thirteen months apart, so I was often asked if they were twins.

I found myself in an emotionally abusive marriage very shortly after having my second son, Chad. I tried to make that relationship work as much as I possibly could. I certainly did not want to be a single mom at twenty-four years of age, but as I saw this turning into a physically abusive situation, I made the decision to leave my husband.

To say he did not make things easy on me would be an understatement. I was only able to escape that home and relationship with the support of my parents. If not for them, I probably would have stayed in that dysfunctional mess of a marriage. There would be years of court battles over support, visitation, restraining orders, and so forth. Unfortunately, my boys were often put in the middle and used as pawns.

I met my second husband, who was five years younger than me, while on vacation in Mexico when I was twenty-eight years old. We married two years later. My young boys instantly felt a strong connection with him. He basically stepped in and became the father they so craved and deserved. He was a very "hands on" stepfather. He did it all: coached their soccer, basketball, and baseball teams. Took them on bike rides, camping trips, you name it. Of course, this made my ex-husband very upset, sparking new problems with him.

We had our daughter, Cassidy, two years later. She was born three months early, so that brought on many, many challenges for our family. I was put on bed rest in the hospital at twenty-one weeks when my water broke. It was extremely difficult to be away from my boys. They were scared, not knowing what was going to happen with me, or with the baby.

My daughter was born at twenty-eight weeks and spent two months in the N.I.C.U. Her brothers fell in love with her despite the nine and ten year age differences.

Chris was in middle school at this point. I definitely was not prepared for the teenage years and what would lie ahead. He started acting out a lot, and was definitely not acting like himself at all. He was surrounding himself with troublemakers, which was very much out of character for him.

My son Christopher was my first love. He was my firstborn, the one who made me a mother. I suppose that's why I felt such a special connection to him. He was a very serious, curious, sensitive child. Growing up, Chris was very well liked by his friends, teachers, and adults. He was practically a straight-A student until the later part of middle school. He loved sports, especially playing football and baseball in his younger years. His favorite football team was the Miami Dolphins, and Dan Marino was his all-time favorite player. He also loved going to Angels games. He played most sports growing up, and was a natural athlete.

We started seeing some minor changes in him at the end of seventh grade when he got into a fight and was suspended from school for a few days. This raised some red flags. I immediately made the decision to switch him to a private school starting in eighth grade in hopes that might be a better setting for him.

The first year of high school, we saw more alarming changes, especially in the friends he was choosing. He started withdrawing from us a bit and his grades began to slip. This is when he first started experimenting with marijuana. He got caught smoking weed in a gas station bathroom next door to the school, and wound up getting suspended for a few days. What was happening to my smart, studious, focused, sensitive boy? After that, he started experimenting with steroids, and eventually got caught selling them at school.

Chris attended a very small private school, so every bout with trouble had to go before the school board. By the grace of God, we were able to keep him in the school, but he had to submit to weekly drug testing and also receive counseling. We thought these actions would bring about positive changes, but he hated going to counseling and withdrew even more.

I knew Chris was still using steroids. I would find them after doing room searches, but even more telling was his personality change. He became very agitated and was not so nice to be around. I remember getting knots in my stomach on my way to pick him up, not knowing what kind of mood he was going to be in. Those days were very tumultuous to say the least—he was disrespectful to his teachers, was drinking, and was not making the best choices in friends. Even so, he was still very much liked by teachers and peers. They all knew he was a good kid, but he was a good kid who made stupid choices.

Chris made it through high school and then went on to a four-year university where he had a decent first semester, but it was the second semester that marked the start of his downfall. I remember being awakened in the middle of the night by police at my front door looking for my son. They told me that his car was involved in a hit-and-run nearby and they were looking for him. He, with a car full of friends, had been speeding through a local neighborhood and crashed into a parked car. Unfortunately, there was someone sitting in that car. Thankfully, the person was not seriously injured, but one of my son's friends in the car *was* hurt, sustaining a broken hip.

Because his friend was injured, Chris was charged with a felony hit-and-run. I knew he just couldn't have a felony on his record; his life would be ruined! But in order to get the felony reduced to a misdemeanor, Chris had to spend thirty days in jail. He also lost his license for one year and was placed on probation. I remember leaving the courtroom early to avoid seeing my baby being handcuffed. I sat in my car and sobbed.

That time in jail, I remember thinking that those were the worst weeks of my life. Thinking of my son sitting in a cell with "real criminals" was too much to bear. We thought—hoped—his spending time in jail would be his rock bottom. We were wrong. He came out of that with an even bigger chip on his shoulder. He also came out of it with a Xanax addiction.

What happened next was an overdose of prescription pills. Chris was very lucky that at least one of his so-called friends cared enough to notice he was turning blue, and dropped him off at the nearest E.R. Getting that call was so scary. We were told he was very lucky, that had he not been brought in he would have died. At this point, I was so very scared for my son—his life was literally spinning out of control and as much as we tried to help him, nothing seemed to work.

For a while, Chris seemed to have gotten back on track. In the six months that had passed since the overdose, he made plans to re-enroll at the university, was working steadily, appeared to be healthy, and was about to get his driver's license back. I was very proud of him and wanted to reward all his hard work. He talked me into buying him a used car, since he would need transportation when he returned to college.

If I could do it all over again, I never would have bought him that car! I have many regrets, and buying him the car is a big one. One month after he got his license back, he got his first DUI. Two months later he would get his *second* one. This was really the beginning of the end for our son.

This time, Chris was sentenced to two months in jail. I would go to visit him every weekend. I would sit across the table from him and see the pain and tears in his eyes. My heart would break into pieces every time as I drove away. His dad and I tried to come together and develop a plan for our son once he got out of jail. I had first thought that the best place for him would be his father's house when he got out of jail. I had two other kids at home, one being a nine-year-old who had already been subjected to so much in her short life. But it soon became clear that his dad was incapable of really helping Chris because his own life was falling apart.

So, we eventually brought him back home with some pretty strict rules in place: he had to get a job and start paying down his hefty court fines, attend his alcohol education classes, and of course, no drug use of any kind would be permitted. He agreed to the terms, and tried very hard to comply.

Then, just before Christmas, Chris had to have his wisdom teeth extracted. I discussed my concerns about Chris receiving any pain medications with his oral surgeon. I was very concerned about the risk of him relapsing. We decided that we would start him on ibuprofen only. If stronger medication was needed, I would administer it.

As planned, I was given the prescription for his Percocet. As we drove home, Chris started flipping out, asking where his medication was and accusing me of withholding it from him. He said he was in a lot of pain and really needed those pills. I was horrified at his anger and so scared.

When we got home, I gave him some ibuprofen and told him to go lie down and sleep it off. That worked for a while, but when he woke up things escalated. He decided to take almost a whole bottle of ibuprofen, and then asked me to take him to urgent care because he thought his stomach was bleeding. He tried everything to get his hands on that Percocet.

I finally realized that Chris knowing the pills were in my possession was just too much for him to handle, and so I got rid of the pills. This whole incident was scary, agonizing, and heartbreaking to witness. It was also another huge wake-up call that my son was not well. I think this story is so important to tell, because I know wisdom teeth extraction is common at this age, and that post-surgical care may involve narcotics, which might lead to serious problems.

By this point, even though our primary rule was that there be no drinking and no drugs, it was just too hard for Chris to live the straight and narrow lifestyle. All he truly wanted was go back to his university and live life as a normal college kid; he didn't understand why he couldn't just be normal. It broke my heart because that was all I wanted for him, too.

But he had so much pain inside. He would say it was because of the divorce fifteen years before, although I didn't buy that explanation at the time. Now, in hindsight, I wonder if all the turmoil his dad had stirred up during his childhood really did have an effect on him psychologically. He never had a great relationship with him. Neither of my boys did.

After a couple of calm months at home, it became clear he wasn't interested in following our rules. He ended up moving in with a friend's mom. He didn't really want to live with this lady, but with her there were no rules. He felt uneasy staying with her and wanted to come home, but he just could not live by our rules.

So, I provided an incentive. I told him if he would enroll in an outpatient drug and alcohol program and prove to us that he was trying, then he could ultimately come back home. Even more importantly for him, he could return to his university.

One morning, when I was planning to pick him up and drive him to his first rehab session, I texted him to say I'd be on my way shortly. He didn't text back. I tried calling, but it went straight to voicemail. I then called the lady he was staying with and asked her to wake him. She called me back, screaming, "Something's wrong with Chris! Chris . . . wake up!" At that moment I froze and immediately went into shock. I knew. This was my biggest fear unfolding: I was going to lose my son.

I told her to hang up and dial 911. I immediately tried to get ahold of my husband, but he was away on business. I did the unthinkable and called my ex-husband. He came and picked me up because I felt paralyzed; I literally could not move. As we drove to the residence where Chris was staying, we had no idea if was dead or alive. We approached the gate to the neighborhood just as the ambulance was exiting. I jumped out to ask the paramedic if Chris was still breathing. He said he was, but just barely.

As we followed the ambulance to the E.R., we had no idea that he was in cardiac arrest. At the hospital, we were informed that they had lost him for about thirteen minutes, but because of his young age they didn't want to give up. They were able to revive him, but thirteen minutes with no oxygen to the brain . . . well I knew what that meant. Because Chris was so young, they wanted to give him every opportunity, so they transferred him to another hospital where they could perform the hypothermia protocol. It's a technique used to lower the body temperature very low to benefit the brain during trauma.

I already knew in my heart that I would never have my Chris back. Not the way he used to be anyway, if at all. He was in the hospital for two days, but his condition worsened almost immediately. It was a complete rollercoaster. His kidneys started to fail, so they put him on dialysis. He had a heart attack, but then his heart function started to improve. One day he had very little brain activity, but the next day it was a little better. Ultimately, though, after all the tests, the doctors told us Chris would not survive this. They told us that we should think about taking him off the life support.

When we removed him from life support, he passed within five minutes. His dad, his brother, and I were with him, holding his hand as he slipped away. I could feel a piece of my own heart leave with him. In a way, though, I felt he had already left long before that moment.

When he was first admitted, we just assumed it was a drug overdose, and that is what we were initially told. He was two weeks shy of his twenty-first birthday; young people that age don't just die. But two months later we received the autopsy report and were shocked to learn that his death was not caused by an overdose! In fact, the toxicology report showed only trace amounts of benzodiazepine and marijuana—certainly not enough to kill him.

No, our son had died due to cardiomegaly, or an enlarged heart. Chris had had a heart attack. After discussing the cause of death at length with the coroner, it was established that he most likely developed an enlarged heart due to his steroid use, although his substance use very likely contributed.

His memorial services were a blur. I honestly don't remember much at all. I will tell you that the church was packed. Someone later said, "You could really see that Chris had two sets of friends." That was true. There were his good friends, the friends he grew up with, his football and lacrosse teammates, teachers, coaches, and all the people that loved him dearly. Then you had the druggies there. They all, both groups, looked up to Chris. But I finally got it—I suddenly understood Chris better. His good friends, like his teammates and other great guys in his life, all loved Chris. But he never felt he was good enough for them; he thought they were all better than him. But his not-so-great friends, the ones who gave him pills, the troublemakers, they all placed him on a pedestal. They all looked up to him, and he loved that. That's where he was most comfortable . . . and that breaks my heart.

I remember being at the cemetery for the burial and watching them lower my son into the ground. It was just family and close friends there. I didn't want to leave. I didn't want to leave my baby boy there, all alone. So, of course I waited and watched as the tractor came to fill up his plot with dirt. I watched them place the grass sod squares over the packed dirt. I wasn't going to leave. Not until it was all finished. I'd brought him into this world; I needed to see him through to the very end.

Exactly one week after his burial was Chris's twenty-first birthday, the birthday he had waited so long for and was so excited about. He had wanted to go to Las Vegas for his twenty-first, but instead we had his birthday celebration at the cemetery. A very dear friend brought food for everyone, some balloons, and a birthday cake. All his friends were there. We all sang Happy Birthday and shared funny Chris stories. It wasn't the twenty-first birthday I had envisioned for my son, but we made the best of it.

Christopher is buried in a beautiful spot overlooking the hills and mountains. It is so peaceful there, and the cemetery is actually a happy place to visit. Loved ones gather and picnic, celebrating their deceased family member or friend. I visited Chris quite often, every Friday morning and, of course, all the holidays. This continued for years. I felt so peaceful and close to him there. Many people would say to me, "He's not there, he's in heaven." But, you know what? That is the body I carried inside and loved for almost twenty-one years. That is a part of him there, and a part of me.

The weeks and months that followed my son's death were so hard. In fact, I struggled for many years trying to redefine myself, to seek answers. I felt lost and I simply did not want to live in a world without my Chris in it. Trying to learn to live without my son here on this earth was unbearably painful. I simply couldn't imagine living the rest of my years without him. But I knew I had other kids who needed me and, I tell you, that is probably the only thing that kept me here.

I went to counseling for months, maybe years, until my therapist told me she could not help me anymore. She told me that I was hanging on to my sadness and thought maybe I would benefit from eye movement desensitization reprocessing (E.M.D.R.) light therapy that can help someone with P.T.S.D. I told her that I didn't want to lose my sadness, that it's my connection to my son. She later told me she understood.

During my struggle with grief I leaned heavily on my faith. During those first days, weeks, months, and even years I can honestly say that there is no way I would have survived without the knowledge I would see my son again. I really sought God out and learned all I could. You name it, I did it. I participated in Bible studies for seven years, although it was more like a Bible *college!* It was very intense but I learned so much during that time.

I found my first parent support group about six months after Chris passed, which happened to be at my church. It took me a while to share my story, but just listening to others was very helpful. Being around others just like me was very comforting. My "normal" friends were there for me in the beginning, but they just didn't really understand what I was going through. I even lost one of my best friends because she just wanted me to be "me" again.

All the things I thought I loved changed. All my priorities changed. I changed. I found great comfort in my support group, and even preferred spending time with them over anyone else. For a time I was involved in several mom grief groups. As I got to know some of the moms in the groups, I was surprised to learn one of their children had been a friend of my son. I found comfort in all my new friendships during this time.

My family struggled. My middle son had enlisted in the Marines, so he left two months after his brother passed away. That was hard, as it felt like I was losing another son. And of course once you lose a child, you are constantly worried about your other children. You think, it happened once, so it can certainly happen again to another child.

We got my daughter into therapy soon after Chris died. She also attended a camp for kids who had lost a sibling or a parent. At home, she felt she couldn't talk to her friends, so she would keep her feelings all bottled up inside, which was not healthy. This wonderful weekend camp was somewhere she could go and connect with others who had experienced a similar loss, and just let it all out.

My husband was my rock. He was always present for me, there for whatever I needed. He gave me my space for about three or four years to do whatever I needed to do. I could not have survived the loss of my son if I hadn't had him.

I am now the facilitator at the support group that I once leaned so heavily on. I find it so therapeutic to be able to talk to the parents who walk through that door, just as I had all those years ago, and to listen to their stories. Just like me back then, I see absolutely no hope in their eyes. But there I am, telling them that they, too, will survive this. I am living proof.

I traveled by myself to Greece and met up with six other grieving moms, whom I didn't know, through a non-profit called Project Grace. We boarded a fifty-two-foot boat and traveled the islands learning about the Greek grieving culture. We took turns telling our story and memorializing each of our children. It was a very humbling and sacred experience.

My husband and I started an endowment scholarship in memory of my son at the university he attended: The Christopher L. Whitman Memorial Scholarship Fund. We were hoping to help students like Chris, young people who had similar interests and goals. Every year, for at least the first six years, they hosted a donor/recipient ceremony and we would drive down to the college and meet the recipient. We really enjoyed doing that as a family.

When you lose somebody so special, like a child, you want to do all you can to keep their memory alive. We have our own special traditions that we keep every year. At Christmas we decorate a small tree out at the cemetery with colored lights. We all go as a family and make a night out of it. We also donate to his scholarship fund on his birthday, his memorial anniversary, and at Christmas. Anything we would have given him, we put into this fund. I still buy him a birthday card every year and write out my heartfelt feelings to him.

As I look back on these past ten years, I have to tell a newly grieving mother that the first year is very tough, going through all the firsts without your child. The second year you are still in that fog and reality sets in, so the second year is almost worse than the first. I felt like even the third year was much the same as the second. But I sensed a shift in my fourth year. I noticed then that I was still here, still breathing, and was surprised to be surviving.

I began to find some happiness in life again. I hate to use the saying "time heals," but in a sense that was how it was for me. You never get over this loss. Your life will never be the same again and you will spend the rest of your life missing, longing for, and loving your child; making sure their memory lives on forever until you take your last breath. If anything, my love for Chris has become more intense.

Just like me, you will figure out a way to move forward through the pain and grief and find your new normal, whatever that may look like. You will go through all the stages of grief. The hardest one for me to get through was the acceptance stage. It was so hard for me to accept the fact that my boy was gone and that I would never see him on this earth, in this lifetime, ever again. I still cannot believe he's gone. Forever.

I'll always have three children. He will always be a part of our family, and I will *always* talk about him. I once read this, and it perfectly describes our relationship now: "Even though your loved one is no longer on this planet in human form, they are still with you and you are very much still in a relationship with them. A new version of relationship is emerging—one based on love, spirit, signs, memories, felt-sense and presence. You don't need to let go . . . you just need to be open to the new ways that the relationship unfolds."

CHAPTER 12

Elizabeth's Story

My name is Elizabeth Moersch, and this is a small bit of my story.

I am a sixty-one-year-old woman who grew up in Orange County, California during the sixties and seventies. Back then the county was filled with new homes, orange groves, eucalyptus tree windrows, and lots of sunshine. I remember the sweet and wonderful smells these trees brought to the air, especially on warm summer nights. It was a beautiful area to grow up in, and for the most part my childhood was carefree and happy.

After finishing school, I traveled a bit and enjoyed my single years living with girlfriends and working as a designer. At twenty-eight I met Peter and, after three years of a fun, active, and love-filled romance, we married. Life was wonderful. Our love story continued and so did our sweet life together. We bought a brand-new home in a neighborhood filled with other new young families, and had three beautiful, healthy, and happy children back-to-back. They were each born nineteen months apart, with Travis born in 1993, Tanner in 1994, and Savannah in 1996.

For the next twenty years, we were a happy family of five. The kids were so close in age that they all had crossover friends, both at school and at church youth group. The boys were best friends and shared a common love of baseball, the beach, and outdoor play in a neighborhood brimming with kids. Wherever the boys were, Savannah was there, too. We were a very close family and loved to play and recreate together. Boating, snow skiing, and adventure type travel vacations were our thing.

My eldest, Travis, was fun, playful, full of joy and was known for his silly jokes and big smile. Travis was a lover of life and lived in gratitude for everything. To know Travis was to love him. He was lovable! He had a servant's heart. He loved sports, the ocean, the river, the mountains and everything about the outdoors. Travis loved, and was deeply attached to, our family, especially his siblings. At a young age he had a great faith and truly wanted to live a life that was pleasing to God. I'm not trying to make him sound perfect, because he wasn't, but he was good.

The years flew by and in the blink of an eye it was June of 2013. It was the 21st, and another school year had just come to an end. It was officially the first day of summer. Travis had two years of undergrad college courses completed by then, and just the day before we had celebrated Tanner's high school graduation. Both boys had been accepted into Texas universities and would be leaving in just a few weeks.

Peter and I thought, "Two down and one to go." Savannah would be entering her senior year of high school in the fall and then all three would be off on their own journey of life. All our summer plans were set. A Hawaiian family vacation was booked, a family portrait was scheduled, and then the road trip to Texas to get the boys settled. It would be a jam-packed summer for sure. Peter and I were proud of each boy and while we knew our family would be changing forever in this new season, we were filled with anticipation and excitement for the future.

That morning, Travis was up early to go to work at the animal hospital. Before leaving, he came into my room to show me the custom Frisbee he had designed online. He had just received it in the mail and told me he was planning to use it later that afternoon at Ultimate Frisbee Friday. He thought the high school kids he mentored would think it was cool. Travis was a Life Group leader for the high school ministry at our church and would often participate in this standing Friday afternoon game. I didn't know it at the time, but that would be our last conversation.

It was around 2:45 p.m. when my phone rang. It was my neighbor, whom I had not seen or talked to in quite a while. She asked where I was, and then proceeded to tell me that Travis had been in an accident and an ambulance was taking him to the hospital. Upon hearing that and the distress in her voice, I panicked! She heard my reaction and then told me Travis was okay and that she would come by to pick me up immediately.

I ran down the stairs and outside to meet my neighbor's car on the street. I immediately tried to call Peter, but he didn't answer. Then my phone rang again. It was Pastor Mike from the church's College Ministry. I yelled, "Mike, is Travis okay?" The other end of the phone was silent. I asked again, "Mike, is Travis okay?" This time he replied, "They are working on him." At that moment I felt my heart sink into my body and the world around me became still and silent. All movement, including my own, seemed to be in slow motion. It felt like I was in a movie. I literally felt my soul leave my body for a second or two. I don't know any other way to describe that moment.

We arrived at the hospital and I noticed an ambulance parked at the entrance to the E.R. The back doors were left open, and the ambulance was empty. I knew it was the ambulance that had carried my boy to this place, and I looked around inside for blood. There wasn't any. At this time, I still did not know what had happened to Travis. I wondered if he had run into the street after the Frisbee and gotten hit by a car. I wondered if he'd fallen down hard and had hit his head. I had absolutely no idea that Travis had gone into cardiac arrest and collapsed on the grassy field where they'd been playing Frisbee. He was gone in an instant and could not be revived.

I entered through the automatic doors to the emergency room and heard someone say, "This is the mother." I kept walking right past triage, the security guard, and about thirty or so crying kids and church pastors that I recognized. I did not stop. Someone from the hospital grabbed my arm and said they would take me to Travis. We went through some double doors and off to the right was a group of doctors surrounding my 6'1", blond-haired, tan, fit, and handsome twenty-year-old son. There lay my baby, my Travis.

At first, I backed away in sheer terror as to what I was witnessing. I then heard a doctor yell, "Clear!" I heard it again, and then a third time. I knew what this meant. My son had died and they were trying to bring him back! At that time someone placed a folding metal chair next to me. I grabbed it and pulled it over as close to Travis as I could get. I stood on it to see over the doctors and yelled, "Travis, you have to come back. You have to come back!" Right then, a hand reached up to grab mine and lower me down from that chair. He was tall and light-haired and looked at me with the most compassionate and sorrowful expression I had ever seen. He shook his head and said to me, "We haven't had a pulse in forty-eight minutes."

The feeling of being in a movie running in slow motion returned and I collapsed in that cold metal chair. My worst nightmare had come true; one of my children had died. My Travis had died! How could this be happening? How could this even be real? I wanted to die myself. How could I live without him?

My memory of the next several minutes as Peter, Tanner, Savannah and the rest of my family arrived is heartbreaking, and perhaps not my story to tell at this time. We were left alone in the room with Travis to say our goodbyes, and we did. We said one final prayer together as a family and, into the Father's hands and our heavenly home, we released our beautiful and precious son, brother, grandson, nephew, and friend.

After Travis died, I did not know how to live or how I could bear the pain of living life without him. I was beyond heartbroken! I was devastated and completely crushed in spirit. The life went out of me. Each day would begin the same. As soon as my eyes opened, Travis would enter my mind and I would burst into tears. This was *not* a dream, and each morning upon waking up, the waves of grief and heartbreak came crashing over me. My body would shake from shock and trauma. The terrible fear I felt from having my world, as I knew it, completely collapse was all consuming.

I realized how very fragile life was. Facing this reality and the fear that something might happen to Tanner or Savannah was debilitating. At this point in time, I still did not know what caused Travis's death. I thought that if it were some inherited cardiomyopathy or something like that, perhaps it might afflict the other kids, too. The fear and anxiety were horrific. I wouldn't take any sedatives or antidepressants because I needed to be alert and get Tanner and Savannah examined and tested. I had to move quickly, especially with Tanner because he was leaving for college.

I was in prayer constantly all throughout the day and night, asking God to protect Tanner and Savannah. I had been a woman of faith for many years and I knew and trusted the word of God. Scripture says, "The spirit of fear does not come from the Lord." (2 Timothy 1:7) I knew my fear was not from God and it was literally killing me physically and mentally. At that time, I was even starting to feel it would be easier to die myself than to live on with this type of fear. So, I got on my knees and said to the Lord, "You are not the author of fear and I will trust you with my life here and now and forever more. Even if my Tanner or Savannah were to go home before me, or should Peter do the same, I will never give up, never lose faith; I will finish my race." As much as saying it still takes my breath away, I meant it. That moment, the fear left and it has never returned. Eventually, we learned that Travis had passed away due to a virus that had injured his heart.

I prayed for God to give me His strength, and I'd ask for His grace to carry me moment by moment. I would not let my mind think too far ahead or let it wander back. I would just stay in the moment and say to myself, "Right here, right now, I'm okay." Someone had tenderly left a tiny book of handwritten Bible verses on my porch and on the cover had written, "For the hard days." The first page read, "The Lord is a strong tower, the righteous run to Him and are safe." (Proverbs 18:10) I would repeat that verse over and over.

In the car, and at night, I would listen to radio programs and podcasts that featured Bible teachings and sermons. All were food for my aching soul. Nothing else would comfort me, only the word of God. His promises, His truths, His strength, and ultimately His good and perfect will for my life were what I yearned for, even if I did not understand it all—and I surely did not!

One overwhelming feeling that kept me going was that of gratitude. I felt so grateful that God had given me a son like Travis and for the amazing life we had all shared together. I was grateful for all my children! They were gifts from God, and I knew it. I'd wanted Travis certainly longer than those twenty years, but if God would let me see into heaven, and find Travis there in the presence of God himself, surrounded by the purest of love and perfection, in a world without sin, would I bring him back? The answer is no, I would not. If God said, "I will roll back time and just give you the two kids, so now you will not have to go through this loss," I would say no! I would not give up one second of Travis's life to spare me this painful journey. So, I remain grateful for the twenty years.

There were so many ways God drew near to my broken heart and showed His faithfulness and love to and for my family and me. These were the moments that kept me going. The scripture "God draws near to the brokenhearted and crushed in spirit" (Psalm 34:18) took on a deeper meaning than I could have ever imagined. Daily, I saw His nearness as He gave me the grace and strength I needed. One day, I was teaching a Bible study on Genesis and came across the scripture, "God breathed life into the man, Adam" (Genesis 2:7). That verse pierced my grieving heart. God was the giver of life and was the breath of that life. One day, that breath will be no more for me, and I, too, will go to heaven, but not yet. I still had breath and knew I had to live and make my life count. I could not throw this gift of life away or back into God's face. I understood clearly that I had to live so I asked God to show me. I mean really, tangibly, show me how. Well, in His faithfulness He did just that.

I remember it was December 2014 and I was out Christmas shopping. I felt broken and fragile and was roaming around the store completely wrapped up in my own thoughts. As many who grieve know, the holiday season can be difficult. As I was browsing the store, I came across a little statue of Mary and Joseph, with baby Jesus cradled in their arms. It was a modern, simplistic statue about five inches tall, and carved out of olive wood. I picked it up and put it back down a few times, and then finally took it to the checkout stand. When I got home, I placed it on my nightstand and I would stare at it as I fell asleep. You see, reflected in that little statue was everything I loved, believed in, and was holding on to. It represented family, love, marriage, beauty, tenderness, and, of course, mother and child. It was holiness, promise, hope, purpose, sanctification, justification, and salvation. It was earthly life and life eternal. Everything that mattered to me was wrapped up in that little statue.

One night I couldn't sleep, so I got up and went downstairs to my garage. I grabbed some paper and a cheap watercolor set from the cupboard and proceeded to paint the image of that little statue. I had never painted before, but that night, and many nights, I painted, pouring out my heart, emotions, and faith onto paper. I felt such tenderness in the silence and solitude of the night. That tenderness, I firmly believe, was the nearness of God. I also felt my Travis, and was often overwhelmed by love and gratitude.

My paintings are simple in style and message. They are colorful and vibrant, reflecting the themes of faith, love, friendship, and family. You do not see brokenness or sadness in them, but rather beauty, love, celebration, and promise.

I went on to reproduce and share my paintings at art shows, galleries, local gift stores and malls, charities, churches, and online. I've sold thousands of prints and paintings, and God has used my art and story over and over to draw others closer to Him. The opportunities to share my art, and the stories of how it has touched someone or how it has been used in some beautiful way, are just extraordinary. One day I will share those perhaps in a future book, but the stories will forever be a source of strength and hope. Every time God uses my art to show His love and tenderness to another or for another, He shows me how to live.

My world changed in an instant when Travis died. My heart broke and it cannot be put back together again. When you have endured this type and depth of loss, there is nothing in *this* world that will suffice. Despite this pain, I live my life with the hope and promise that I will see Travis again one day in heaven. I remain ever so grateful to have been his mother here on earth. There has been no greater gift or honor in my life.

Today, Travis would be twenty-eight and most likely be finished with veterinary school and doing what he loved, working with animals and their people. While I will never stop yearning for my sweet Travis, and every day still has a teary moment or two, I keep my eyes on the Lord and I believe His promises. As my husband often reminds me, especially on the hard days, "We are one day closer." Until then, I live. I live for God, for Travis, for my family, for love of others, and for you. I will never give up. I will never lose faith. I will finish my race.

His Grace is sufficient!

Tenderly,

Elizabeth

Elizabeth Moersch Studios:
https://www.facebook.com/elizabethmoerschstudios

CHAPTER 13

Janice's Story

Hello, my name is Janice, and this is my story. On March 18th, 2021, our family marked the nine-year anniversary since our beloved Tyler left this challenging world to join his Father, our Lord, in heaven. I am a wife, a mother, and am still working as a front-end manager at a local grocery store. Each day I do what I can to make sure that the tragedy of my son's death does not have the final say over the love that continues to live on. He is here in the song of a bird, the wind on my face, and the stars in the sky. He is here in the raindrops falling, the rustle of a leaf, and the clouds floating softly in the sky. He is forever with me because I carry him in my heart; love lives on in spite of death. This can only be understood when you are filled with the holiness of the Spirit and the power of His love from within. God helps me to see my son daily in His creation.

I was raised in a very strict and good Catholic family. A Catholic family upbringing entailed a Catholic education, going to church every Sunday, and religion taught as a subject in school. I always knew the Lord, but on That Day I realized I hadn't truly *known* Him until the moment I lost my son. I seriously depended on Him with every breath I took. He saved me from the lifelong prison I had been thrown into, a prisoner with no knowledge or understanding of what happened or why I had to now live on without Tyler. In that prison I have flailed in an abyss of shock, terror, panic, heartache, and utter hopelessness. This prison is called the loss of a child.

Tyler was my baby, my third born and youngest son of three. He lived only a very short time, just twenty-five years. His childhood days were fun-filled and simple. An extremely active child he was, always needing something to do. His life was joyful, spending time playing with his special childhood friends and playing competitive sports. Tyler had deep and meaningful connections with certain friends. His was a happy childhood, filled with making endless memories with his two brothers and his friends.

Of my three boys, raising Tyler was a little more challenging. He seemed to need more attention and interaction than his brothers had. He always needed reassurance, to be understood, to be recognized and loved. His character was that of a pleaser, always wanting to do a good job. Being the youngest, Tyler was a bit more temperamental, wanting to get his own way and causing a fuss if he didn't. Still, he always had such a big, loving heart. I saw no real struggles in him as a young boy, nothing out of the ordinary.

Tyler was popular at school, had girlfriends, and one girlfriend in particular whom he cherished. Throughout his entire life, including high school, he was always very involved with sports. During his senior year, I noticed he had acquired a problem with alcohol, and I became worried when I saw he wasn't able to control it. Aside from the drinking problem that had developed, Tyler's life up until high school graduation was normal.

Tyler went on to take general education classes at a local community college for a year, but eventually decided he was better suited to working. He didn't think he was as smart as his high-achieving friends, so instead of the college track, he decided to take a job at his dad's pool cleaning business, a business my husband has owned for thirty-five years. Tyler had fifty pools on his route, and was a responsible, hard-working young man.

While some of his friends were working toward specific goals, Tyler really had no set direction yet. He was a simple kind of guy. He told me once he didn't feel like he belonged in this era. He wished for a simple life, like back in the sixties when the husbands put in a hard day's work at the factory, had a couple of kids and a dog, went out on Saturday nights, and washed the cars on Sunday. Just a simple life.

Sadly, Tyler's drinking became a worsening problem, so at this point of his story I would like to discuss stigma. Stigma is a mark of disgrace that sets a person apart from others. People look down on people who struggle with substance problems. They assume they became addicted to alcoholic or a drug by choice, that it was the person's own fault. When you are labeled in this way, you are no longer seen as an individual but as a part of a stereotyped group.

But really, what does the "normal" person know about addiction and its consequences if they have not encountered the problem in someone they know? Unless they personally know someone who has suffered from this disease, a friend or someone in their own family, how could they understand it? Back then, I certainly did not.

I couldn't even reveal to my mom or my sisters and brother what had happened to my own son for a very long while. Although I'm sure they all suspected Tyler had a problem, we all chose to remain silent. I felt they just wouldn't understand, and I refused to let anyone think or speak badly of my son.

During the course of his five to six-year battle with alcohol, I became the "enabler mom." I tried to fix everything, always thinking that he would get over it, that it was just a phase he was going through, and so on. Deep inside, though, I knew he had a bigger problem than what my husband and I had been telling ourselves. I had no idea how to cope with Tyler's alcoholism. I couldn't even reveal his problem to my closest friends. I kept it all bottled up inside. I was in a prison all by myself, and because my husband just could not see Tyler's situation clearly.

Sadly, I believe the stigma will always exist. Still, my hope is that, little by little, people will begin to recognize and understand all the many facets to this incredibly disabling illness that may someday affect a loved one or family member. To get beyond stigma, people need to have love, empathy, and compassion to be able to grasp the pain and comprehend the extreme difficulties they face each and every day. I still have a hard time with this issue. I am still angry about it. Will I ever not be? Trying to be there for someone with an addiction is exhausting at times, and sometimes you just have to choose a different path for the sake of your own mental health.

Tyler's alcoholism resulted in some harsh consequences. With two D.U.I.s and a two-month stay in jail, he came out of jail no better than when he went in. Countless A.A. meetings and so many other commitments, like court-appointed meetings, made it impossible for him to live a normal life. But still, according to him, he had no problem, so there was no accountability.

Because Tyler had no car to get around in, there I was . . . rowing the boat, again and again. We had entered a very dysfunctional relationship. Although, looking back, I am not sure how long we were like this—maybe always. About this time, drugs surfaced, too, further complicating the worsening situation.

As a child, Tyler had never shown any signs of mental illness. But after his misuse of OxyContin, his brain changed. That drug totally changed him. He was not the son I knew or had parented. People debate about which comes first: substance abuse or the mental health problem. I don't believe we will ever know that answer. He started struggling with anxiety, which I believe was directly related to the drugs. Oxy made him act crazy; it literally changed his brain. I believe that when you let drugs in, you also open that door to Satan allowing him to advance against us, to gain more ground, and to destroy our lives. While in the throes of addiction, that sin gives the evil one a place to cultivate confusion and injure your soul. *"Be alert and of sober mind. Your enemy the devil prowls around like a roaring lion looking for souls to devour"* —1 PETER 5:8

I would refer to Oxy as The Beast of Burden. He soon found himself in the grip of this opioid. I don't quite remember how he got to that point, but does it matter? It happened; addiction had reared its ugly head. I became the crazy mom, snooping through his room, rummaging through drawers and his closet and throwing away any hidden alcohol or items that shouldn't be there. I would read his text messages on his phone, then track down his drug dealers and threaten them. Yes, I was crazy and I was determined to save my son!

I literally had no idea what to do, so I became the "tough love" mom. I told him he could no longer live with us. I couldn't go on that way anymore and began to realize my part in the crazy merry-go-round type of life we'd created. I honestly hoped that, by being away from home, he might change his perspective. So he moved to Arizona to live with his brother. At this time, before he moved away, he fathered a child, although he had no parental rights or commitments. Sadly, the mother and Tyler were even more dysfunctional and alarming when together. Fire on fire is never a good combination. As the saying goes, two birds of a feather flock together. And so, the saga continued.

Nearly a year went by. One day he called me and said he wanted to come home to be near his child. I gave him an ultimatum, telling him flatly, "No, not unless you go to rehab and figure out yourself and your life." I knew he was still drinking and had not embraced sobriety in any way. During the year he lived out of state, I had worked on myself and had changed. I was no longer willing to be engaged in his decisions. My mind grew healthier as I took responsibility for my own bad behavior during his addiction. I used to wonder, "When do parents stop trying to do things for their children?" and now I knew. The time was now.

A few weeks later Tyler came home, agreeing to enter the Teen Challenge treatment program. After spending three months there, his brother arranged for him to transfer to a nearby sober living home in San Diego. He lived and worked there for nine months. We were so proud of his progress! Because of the pending court case concerning his parenting rights, we allowed him to come home and live with us as long as he was working and sober. He lived with us a mere three months before the tragic day arrived.

When you receive that horrible phone call, you surely believe it is the worst day of your life. But is it? Every day since that call has been a nightmare and I wonder, when am I going to wake up? Shock. Anger. Denial. Brokenness. All of these emotions overwhelmed me.

It was 6:00 am on a Saturday morning. The phone rang and a frantic woman, the mother of one of Tyler's friends, was screaming at me to "come right away"—that my son was in cardiac arrest. I hurled the phone. My husband flew out the door and immediately drove over to the house, which was close by. I was frantically running around the house for no apparent reason, then dropped, frozen on the floor, and sat there screaming up to God, "Please, *please* dear God, don't take my son!" Over and over I was praying, begging, pleading, and bargaining with God, but somehow, deep down, I knew that he was gone. And he was.

Taken away by ambulance, after continuous C.P.R. efforts, my son was transported by the first responders to Mission Hospital, the hospital where he was born and where he would now be pronounced deceased. They didn't know the cause of death at the time, no one did. We believed he was sober now, so what happened? Did he have a bad heart? We would have to wait a couple of months for an autopsy report to find the answers about why Tyler died. There with him at the hospital, I could feel his energy was gone. Never had I ever felt that feeling before, an eerie sense of emptiness.

The day after his passing, an amazing thing happened. Morning had come, yet the fogginess of what had occurred lingered. I woke up and opened the garage door, standing there holding a cup of coffee. I looked up at the sky and started praying and talking to God, asking Him if He had Tyler with Him. I knew He did but I needed assurance. As I spoke I then directed my thoughts to Tyler and yelled up at him, "Tyler, are you with the Lord? I know you are but I need a sign to know for sure. Tyler, please send me a sign, anything, I just need to know."

As I stood outside looking up, I was hoping to see his face, or some kind of sign, but did not see anything. I then said out loud, "I believe that God will allow you to do that, so I am not leaving until you send me a sign." A few minutes later, suddenly I began to see tiny bubbles floating down from above. They start to encircle me, some popping, some big, some small. They soon surrounded and enveloped me with such a powerful sense of peacefulness and love. I could *feel* it, there was just so much love.

No words can describe the sense of pure love and peacefulness that I felt in those few minutes of glory. I knew it was God's presence! I was joyous as I stood there thinking of the Bible verse that says: "Then you will experience God's peace and understanding, which exceeds anything we can understand. His peace and love will guard your hearts and minds as you live in Christ Jesus." I experienced just this. "Thank you, God, thank you, Tyler. You are with the Lord and you are so happy."

That was the first of many, many signs I received from Him. I was a little confused at first about who was giving me these signs, but only God can do miracles. All that week my family and I received "Tyler signs." Two days later, a beautiful mallard duck appeared in my backyard. He came by many times a week to visit, and I grew to become friends with that duck. The last day he visited us was on Father's Day.

Finally, the day arrived when we received the report from the coroner's office. As I read it, tears, tears, and more tears rolled down my face. The report stated that the cause of Tyler's death was due to the combined effects of alcohol and methadone. It made no sense to me, especially because the amounts registered in his body were very minimal. And methadone? I knew nothing about this particular drug. I learned later that it's a drug used for helping people recover from an opioid or heroin addiction. People don't die registering these levels, but I guess the mixing of alcohol with the methadone was deadly. The saying that "one pill can kill" is true.

It felt like my heart was ripped out of my body. No way did he die like this. A darkness, and so many questions, plagued my mind, my heart, and soul. I never dreamed I would lose a child from this senseless affliction. Was this shame that I felt? And how did this happen? Was this my fault? Was I not a good mother? What did I do wrong? All these questions were swimming around in my head.

I was filled with desperation and called out to God to send me my duck. He hadn't been here at the house for a long while. Well, God answered my call immediately! My beautiful mallard duck flew in, landing loudly on top of our pool and with a graceful glide. Seeing the duck arrive like that shook every fiber in me. God filled my heart with the Holy Spirit. I felt a peaceful calm come over me and could hear Him speaking to my heart. God wanted me to know that, "His death does not define him. I got this! Death is not a punishment. He is with me."

For several years, I felt I was in another world. I kept my eyes focused on "up above," not in the earthly place in which I lived. How did I survive the loss of my child? For me I can only say it was my strong faith in God. I totally surrendered to Him. By doing this, God's love, presence, strength, and incredible peace helped stabilize my heart and allowed me to get through each moment as it occurred. I also discovered the Solace group, led by Maggie Fleitman, a gathering of mostly women who were all amazing and brave. I attended Solace meetings for four years. Parents there were able to share their personal nightmares together, each with different stories, different scenarios. I knew I was not alone, that we had each other.

In addition to the Solace group, my friends, family, and a Bible study group were also of great support. Finally, attending Saddleback Church, which I had been a member of for over thirty years, helped me stay in reverent communication with our Lord and Savior.

I was determined to keep Tyler's memory alive. I kept a journal about my grief journey and my deep love for Tyler. I took pictures of every sign I got from Heaven, to record them so I would never forget. These little signs helped to keep me alive, showing me that our spirit and soul lives on, that I will see him soon. Death is not the end, but a beginning of a new and perfect world with our Lord and Creator.

I am blessed to have a close relationship with my grandchild, a wonderful gift that Tyler left us. Part of my son will always be alive in my grandchild, and I will keep his memory alive by chatting about Tyler, by saying his name.

I also set up a Facebook memorial page for family and friends to post little messages to him and to honor his memory. I also found, as a grieving mother, that I could help other mamas who had lost their child, so I'd offer my encouragement, hugs, and support to be there for them during their dark moments.

At the end of the day, as my eldest son once wrote, and which has always resonated with me, "Although some wounds never heal, we learn to cherish our scar." I also remember reading something that has helped me remain healthy mentally. It went something like this:

After almost a decade now, sometimes it doesn't feel like a knife anymore or that I have a life sentence of misery. Sometimes it feels like a fact, and it intensely sucks and the thought hurts like hell. On big occasions, that fact is just harder to hold and you have to pick up the pieces one by one. BUT the fact also means that life has come from death, that out of sorrow was borne beauty, and the impact of his life was not confined to the mere moments he had breath in his lungs. Because the fact is. . . love is greater and still wins no matter how hard death tries to diminish it.

Grief is always present. Some days are like puffy clouds passing by, as I remember the treasured moments and pine for a future that was not meant to be. Other days, there are only dark storm clouds, and the blackness is truly menacing. And that is okay, too, as long as you don't sit in the darkness for too long.

PART TWO

Healing

CHAPTER 14

Restoration Project Underway

If you are a mother who has suffered the loss of a child, you are probably a crumpled mess, feeling utterly depleted in the aftermath of the death. Saying goodbye to your son or daughter is like chopping off a limb or cutting out your heart. Sorrow then seems to permeate what's left of you, leaving behind a broken and dusty shadow of who you once were.

While all that may be true for a period of time, it is, fortunately, not a permanent condition! Deep inside each grieving mother remains a stubborn desire to survive. We may never be the same, but we are still here. Eventually, that survival instinct rises up and makes itself known. We decide, begrudgingly, that we really do want to keep on living.

When you do finally emerge from the catacombs of sorrow, you will begin to realize there are people in your life who need you, who depend on you, and who love you. They, too, want to see you survive the tragic loss. These loved ones care about your quality of life and are probably very concerned about your mental state and overall wellbeing. No one can begin to imagine the pain you are in, and most won't even try, but they love you and want you back.

When it dawns on you that your own suffering is also reverberating through those closest to you, it can be both endearing and annoying. Endearing because you are very touched to see how much your family and friends love you, but annoying because it feels like they are applying some subtle, or not so subtle, pressure to "get over it." If there is one bit of advice I can offer other grieving mothers, it is to not allow anyone to pressure you to bounce back on their desired timetable. If they truly love you, they will be patient and allow the process to unfold organically.

However, if you try to see yourself through their eyes, you can begin to understand why they might be concerned about you. For example, you may have spent the last few months eating poorly. Grief can cause you to lose your appetite—at least it had that effect on me. When I did get around to eating, it was usually frozen meals or taking shortcuts, such as having a bowl of cereal for dinner. You just don't feel like making the effort to feed yourself, and nothing sounds very appetizing anyway.

Maybe you have given up your usual physical activities, languishing zombie-like on the couch under a blanket instead. Again, it is hard to muster up the gumption to put on your sneakers and exert yourself when you have no desire to take care of your health. You just have zero motivation.

Possibly you have not been getting enough quality sleep. Sleep becomes elusive for us who grieve, even though we crave it so badly. In fact, sleep is the only thing we actually look forward to, as it promises us a respite from the feelings that eat us up all day long. Even so, you might toss and turn for hours, still processing in your mind the tragic loss and all the events surrounding the death. Slumber simply evades you, no matter how much you need and want a good night's sleep.

Sleep issues cut both ways, however. Some may find themselves wanting to do nothing *but* sleep. Sleep serves a dual function while in grief mode. The emotional strife can literally wipe a person out. Sleep helps to replenish all that used up energy. But sleep can also function as an escape from the sad reality that is too hard to face. It isn't surprising at all that people who are grieving a significant loss may sleep excessively, a condition called hypersomnia.

Then, of course, your state of mind may be concerning. Loved ones may be worried about your mood swings, expressions of anger, extreme fatigue, or feelings of failure and guilt. You may be sleep-walking your way through each day, unable to feel anything at all.

The symptoms I have just described also happen to be classic signs of depression.

You have just gone through a devastating life event. In the early days and weeks following the loss of your son or daughter, you are in shock, you are depressed, and you may even be traumatized. As awful as it feels, know that this condition is not static, that it will change with the passage of time. Regardless of how badly your loved ones want to see you rebound, honor yourself by ignoring any pressure and allow yourself the needed time to restore your wellbeing.

You are now officially what I refer to as a restoration project. You are under construction—undergoing an organic renovation with no set completion date. Just as you wouldn't want to rush a home remodeling project and end up with a shoddy result, you certainly shouldn't rush the remodeling project that is *you*. You need the precious gift of time to get your legs back under you. So, put up the scaffolding and mesh fencing and stake out your boundaries. Your loved ones will just have to understand that you feel crushed at the moment and need sufficient time to be able to build yourself back up.

How much time, exactly? No two grieving mothers will heal in the same way or within the same timeframe. There are many factors that affect our resilience in trying times. By nature, each of us has unique personality traits and temperaments that influence how we respond to setbacks, frustration, disappointment, and, yes, loss. No two people are wired the same, so no two mothers will rebound from their terrible loss in quite the same way.

Even the way we work through our restoration process can be vastly different when comparing one mother to another. Some women might be able to compartmentalize their pain and function at a higher level after losing a child. People may look at these mothers and be in awe of their strength. However, be aware that this might actually be a smoke screen, a type of coping mechanism that only camouflages what is going on under the hood. In time, even for these super strong women, the grief will have its day.

And then there are some mothers who spend the next six months in their pajamas after losing a son or daughter, and that's okay, too. Again, each woman is hardwired in her own way. Remind yourself, there is a reason it is referred to as a grieving *process*.

While you are nursing your broken heart, there are some things you can do to assist the progress of your restoration project:

STAY CONNECTED

If you have recently suffered the loss of your child, you may first reject my suggestion to stay connected to family and loved ones as you crawl out of the black hole of grief. I absolutely get it! When I suggest you remain connected, I am referring to a little later on when you begin to see some signs of life in yourself again. If you are anything like me, the very last thing you want to do is socialize with anyone. In fact, I clearly remember feeling utterly exhausted after attempting to have lunch with a girlfriend. It took every ounce of my energy to pretend I was just a normal person having lunch at a restaurant, when in reality I was a total mess underneath the fake smile plastered on my face. Take all the time you need before stepping back into a social situation.

That being said, it is very, very important to not become a self-isolating recluse for an extended period of time. At some point, say within the first three months following the death, do try to visit with a close friend, a parent, or a sibling—even sooner if you feel up to it. From my own experience, I would suggest you start very small, such as having a friend over for a cup of tea or to take a walk. A public setting puts too much pressure on you to put up a strong front. Being close to home with just one or two people gives you the freedom to express your grief without worrying what the waiter is thinking.

Again, because everyone deals with grief in their own way, some mothers may be very comfortable returning to social situations, even small gatherings with friends or coworkers, early on. There is no right or wrong way to manage your social life following the loss of a child. But just know that it is essential that you don't cut off all those who love you, as that will only add to the feelings of loss in your life. You will actually need their support more than you could imagine when you first began the grief journey. Connection to loved ones is likely to become your lifeblood eventually.

For sure we do experience a strange dichotomy in those early months after our child's passing. Never have we felt so alone, although some of our loneliness is actually self-imposed. Be aware that part of the resistance you experience regarding reconnecting with friends may stem from an assumption that they just cannot relate to you now. You may worry that you'd make your friends or coworkers feel awkward or uncomfortable in your presence. This is a legitimate concern. What you have suffered through is unimaginable to others. In fact, it scares them because it stokes a subliminal fear that if it happened to you it might happen to them. People sometimes do struggle when encountering a person who has recently lost a child. They may fear they'll say something that might make the mother feel worse, or even anger her.

In my personal experience after losing Matthew, my friends didn't really avoid me, but some seemed a bit tentative around me at first. I admit that picking up that vibe did hurt a bit. I already felt like an odd duck, self-conscious about my son's suicide. But even so, on some level I understood their discomfort. I would probably feel a little awkward, too, if I was in the same situation as the onlooker. Still, try not to project your own pain onto your friends, as that may prevent you from spending time with them.

Dip your toe, little by little, back into the world of the living, first with phone conversations, then a meet-up or two with your closest friends, and eventually a social setting such as a smallish family gathering. Never push yourself to move faster than is comfortable, and mind your gut feeling about which settings work for you and which ones might trigger you.

STAY ACTIVE

I don't know about you, but when I am depressed the last thing I want to do is go to the gym and work out. It is kind of a cruel joke, because in that thick, incapacitating fog of sorrow there is little gumption to physically exert yourself, when in reality being active is very helpful when struggling with depression. When we exercise our brain releases endorphins. These are the feel-good chemicals that act like a magic mood booster while also mitigating stress. Physical activity also stimulates neurotransmitter production, releasing serotonin, dopamine, and norepinephrine. These brain chemicals also help to regulate stress, improve mood, and contribute to better sleep quality.

Your willingness to be active during the early phase of grief is probably going to be influenced by whether exercise was part of your regular routine before the loss. Women who were accustomed to being physically active will have an easier time reintroducing exercise into their lives than those who hadn't been particularly active. Regardless, all you grieving mothers should try to incorporate some exercise into your weekly routine.

Keep in mind that a fitness routine is whatever you want it to be. Whether you like to run, hike, swim, cycle, dance, walk, or paddleboard does not matter at all. Just pick a couple of activities that you will stick with and integrate them into your life. You will find yourself feeling more energetic, less depressed, cognitively sharper, and getting better sleep as a result. Also, by keeping a consistent exercise routine—and I actually schedule my workouts into my calendar so they become integral to my daily tasks—you'll notice some nice physical improvements. Seeing your body get stronger and more toned gives you a little boost in confidence at a time when you need it most.

Some moms may take this to a higher plateau, as with Evan's mom, Gina. Gina made a decision to not only get physically toned and healthy, but to actually set aggressive fitness goals. She wanted to compete. So, Gina joined a boot camp, hired a trainer, and began serious weight training. Soon, she set her sights on the Spartan Races and, by gosh, she did it, mud, injuries, and all.

IMPROVE YOUR DIET

There's a reason why yummy, fattening, satisfying foods are called "comfort foods." These are the food choices we reflexively make when we are going through a difficult emotional chapter in our lives because, news flash, they make us feel better. Often there is a bit of nostalgia attached to these foods, as they tend to be the treats or meals we enjoyed when we were young. There is absolutely nothing wrong with indulging in comfort foods for a while following a terrible and traumatic life event like the loss of your child.

However, there is a limit to the benefits derived from devouring Cheetos or fried chicken or chocolate cake. Eventually, these foods will turn on you, should you allow poor food choices to become a new habit. And being at a low point in your life anyway, the resulting weight gain, ruddy complexion, and low energy will only make you feel worse. So go ahead and treat yourself to some otherwise no-no foods for a bit, but only in moderation.

More and more evidence is pointing to nutrition as having a powerful effect on our mental health. There is ample science showing how nutrition impacts our wellbeing. Healthy food choices help maintain balanced sugar levels in the blood, maintain a healthy gut biome, and improve brain function, but all the science can be reduced to a very simple message: Your body needs certain nutrients to feel better and to function at an optimal level.

Consider these dietary tips:

- *Foods rich in omega-3 fatty acids.* Omega-3 fatty acids have powerful health benefits for heart health, reducing inflammation, and optimizing brain function. These foods include salmon, Brussels sprouts, avocados, walnuts, flaxseeds, berries, chia seeds, edamame, and tuna.
- *Leafy greens and fresh fruit.* For high vitamin content and fiber, enjoy lots of salads using spinach, kale, watercress, arugula, and romaine. Include multiple servings of fresh fruits and veggies in your daily diet, too.
- *Whole grains.* Select high quality whole grain breads, pastas, and cereals.

- *Low-fat dairy.* Opt for low-fat Greek yogurt, milk, and cheeses.
- *Healthy fats.* Use olive oil, canola oil, or safflower oil in your salads and cooking.
- *Limit sugar.* An occasional treat is fine, but do limit your sugar intake for optimum health.

AVOID SUBSTANCES

We are all familiar with the phrase "drowning your sorrows" as it relates to using the comforting effects of alcohol while winding through a terribly depressing chapter of life. While a glass of wine can provide a warm, relaxing effect, too much alcohol can end up making things much worse.

Alcohol use disorder tends to creep up on a person. Abusing alcohol for an extended period of time, in hopes of numbing the pain in your sad heart, can result in an alcohol problem before you even realize what happened. Even if you do not develop an alcohol use disorder, alcohol can still have a negative effect on you. It can lead to weight gain, puffiness, low energy, hangovers, and disrupted sleep. If you are already depressed, excessive alcohol consumption will only exacerbate the symptoms of depression.

This same advice holds true for any substance that might be used to self-medicate your way through a painful time. Benzodiazepines, the sedatives sold under the brand names of Xanax, Ativan, and Valium, are extremely addictive. This happens quickly as tolerance to the effects of these drugs increases and you end up taking higher or more frequent doses than what was prescribed by the doctor. Once you become dependent on benzodiazepines, and then want to stop taking the drug, the withdrawal effects can be downright dangerous.

The bottom line is, other than for providing some temporary psychological relief immediately following the death of a child, all substances should be either avoided entirely or only used occasionally. If you have a history of a substance use disorder, you should avoid all substances, period.

SEEK SUPPORT

Navigating the horrible grief that follows the loss of a child is extremely difficult. While true that it is possible to do this on your own using raw inner strength, lots of courage, and some well-honed coping skills, for most of us the grief process can definitely be aided by the guidance of a trained grief counselor.

Grief therapy involves meeting with a mental health professional on a regular basis, usually once a week, so you can discuss your emotional status. Personally, I know how much I benefited from the help of a lovely grief counselor for about a year following my two back-to-back losses. I will go into this topic more thoroughly in an upcoming chapter.

These skilled clinicians offer a comforting space where you can share your deepest emotions without exposing yourself to judgment or expectations. For me, my weekly hour with a therapist was a bright spot during an otherwise dismal weekly routine. I always looked forward to spending that hour talking about my son and my man, sharing memories about them while plowing through her handy box of tissues as I sobbed my eyes out.

Some grief therapists will assign reading materials or ask you to write an occasional short essay about some aspect of your grief process. Some will just sit quietly after delivering a prompt or asking a question that you are to mull over and respond to. Some may utilize cognitive behavioral therapy to help you examine faulty thought patterns that might be keeping you stuck in your grief. Some may use exposure therapy if the child's death was traumatic. Although the techniques may differ, the purpose of grief therapy is to provide a safe outlet for your sorrow as you wind through the stages of grief.

Ultimately, each mother's restoration project will last as long as it needs to. Allow yourself the time and space to adequately attend to your own needs while you nurture your broken heart. Slowly but surely, with some self-love and patience, you will return to the land of the living . . . albeit in a profoundly changed form.

CHAPTER 15

Spirit in the Sky

Everyone, whether they are a mother or not, will at some point in their lives have to access certain coping skills to manage the debilitating effects of grief. No one gets to sidestep this one. When it's our turn to suffer through a significant loss, we will all cope in our own unique ways.

Women who have experienced the gut-wrenching loss of a child must dig really deep to muster the strength to get through each and every day. You have no doubt noticed, as you read the stories relayed by these brave mothers, a common thread running through them. Just as I did, they, too, leaned on strong faith beliefs to survive the pain of profound loss.

Developing a faith in something greater than our self is a very personal journey. Each person's belief system is uniquely their own, built upon three layers—things they've been taught, things they've read, and things they've experienced in this life—plus a huge dose of blind faith. When tragedy strikes, turning to our faith as a source of comfort is quite a natural inclination.

Personally, I am a Catholic revert, meaning I was a cradle Catholic who left the religion of my childhood for over two decades before returning to the Church in 1998 at age forty-two. Looking back, I can see now how God put a plan in place for my life. He led me back to the church of my childhood knowing full well what lay ahead in my future. He knew that I would need Him. I have no doubt that my strong faith has sustained me through the loss of my son, and then Mike, and all the emotional devastation that followed.

But my "spirit in the sky" may look vastly different from another mother's. Women from all faith beliefs lose children. Whether these mothers practice a formal religion like Catholicism, a mainline Protestant denomination, or the Jewish faith, or if they are drawn toward an evangelical or non-denominational faith practice, is not material. The common thread that connects us is the belief that there is a God and that He loves us and is watching over us—*and* our child—as we grieve.

Many women may consider themselves spiritual in other ways. These mothers may have a strong spiritual connection through nature. In this way they may gain comfort from God indirectly, such as through His beautiful natural creations. This type of spirituality—the song of a bird, the smell of the ocean, the beauty of a rose—provides some measure of peace to their broken hearts.

As well, there are mothers who don't particularly have a defined faith, or may even lack any faith at all. For these women I can only pray that they keep seeking. I believe it would be much more difficult to survive the heartbreak of losing a child without faith. That said, no one should impose his or her own faith beliefs on a grieving mother, as tempting as it is, even when coming from a place of pure compassion. There might be a sincere desire to direct the mother toward God, but in her time of deep grief she may not be receptive to the gesture. In fact, it could result in hurt feelings or misunderstandings, or even harm the relationship.

As a Christian, of course I want everyone to know Jesus and believe in His teachings. But I have also been on the other side during the decades I referred to myself as agnostic. No one could reach me during the years when I was closed off to religion. Indeed, it is usually a mistake to push your faith beliefs on someone at such a raw time. Instead, just pray for them. Pray for their sad heart to be soothed. Pray for them to find strength. And, of course, it is always good to pray that they may someday find their way to God.

For the grieving mothers who do have a strong faith belief, this is the time to lean on it. I discovered the daily devotional, *Jesus Calling*, in the early days of my grief work. I highly recommend this amazing little book. Friends were very generous and showered me with beautiful little prayer books and trinkets, which helped me to increase my trust in God while aiding my journey toward acceptance.

Special Catholic devotions have been a significant source of spiritual nourishment for my broken heart, especially after the first year or so was behind me. Reading about the saints will always offer perspective with regard to suffering. There are novenas, the nine days of prayer to seek special graces, just for parents who have lost a child. I pray the rosary daily, a practice I have maintained for over twenty years, while on my walks. Another source of solace for me has been the hour I spend each week in Eucharistic Adoration at my church. In Adoration I literally become like a little child, sitting in the small chapel and soaking up God's love. Also, when I travel I make a point to visit the beautiful churches I pass, stopping in to light a candle and say a prayer for my boy.

After some time has passed, you, too, might find yourself drawn deeper into your devotional life. You may seek answers from spiritual reading materials, including taking a deeper dive into the Bible. You might consider joining a ministry at your place of worship, a Bible study, a small group, or attending a workshop. Women's retreats are also a wonderful way to nurture your broken heart and seek affirmation when you are ready to be a bit more social.

Allow your faith to deepen and evolve as you wind through the grief journey. This can deliver huge rewards, as I have found in my own faith walk. I discovered a women's group at my church called Endow that has become so very special to me. These women have provided much needed spiritual and emotional support to me, as well as a loving fellowship, over the years since losing my son and Mike.

Even with a strong faith, however, I admit I have had some very dark days and weeks. No matter how fervent my beliefs, the fact remains that my son is gone. This beautiful human being who was flesh of my flesh is no longer on the planet. The pain that emanates from that awful fact is very real. Jesus can't take away this earthly human pain.

People have wondered how I can still believe in a God who would allow such tragedies to occur. In all these seven years, only once did I experience anger toward God. It was the year after Mike's death, and I was visiting his grave on what would have been his fifty-seventh birthday. As I sat there at the grave, I soon found myself lying flat on my back staring up at the sky, tears flowing. A sudden wave of anger shot through me, and the next thing I knew I was shouting, loudly, toward the heavens, "WHY DID YOU TAKE HIM FROM ME?"

As much as we would all love to avoid pain and suffering, the reality is that God never promised us heaven on earth—well, okay, maybe *before* the Fall. After that event, the stage was set for the possibility of any sorrow or misery that can befall a living human being. Still, my faith keeps me grounded in the belief that there is a heaven and the hope that I will be reunited with my loved ones one day. Until then, I will try to keep my eyes firmly fixed on Christ and trust that He has my back. Jesus, I trust in You.

> "So do not fear, for I am with you; do not be dismayed, for I am your God. I will strengthen you and help you; I will uphold you with my righteous right hand"
>
> —Isaiah 41:10

CHAPTER 16
Mind Over Matter

In the first year or two following Matthew's death I must admit I was pretty much a hot mess. I really was. I had a unique situation, as I shared earlier, in that I didn't have the luxury of tending to my grieving heart in any real way after my son's totally shocking and unexpected suicide. I was caring for Mike during his leukemia journey and needed to be strong for him. Many times, though, that sure didn't go as planned. I clearly remember driving him to the hospital for a transfusion a few months after Matt died, and a car cut in front of us on the freeway. While encountering a rude driver on the road might normally be simply annoying, that day I began to shake and become very unstable at the wheel. I was obviously in P.T.S.D. mode and any little thing that startled me seemed to cause an intense reaction.

I remember when the social worker assigned to Mike came to his hospital room to discuss his needs and the post-stem cell transplant caregiving responsibilities with me. When she learned that I had recently lost my son, she became very concerned about my ability to manage the stress of caring for a transplant patient. Rightly so! I ended up convincing her that I would be able to manage it, but she did recommend that I receive some psychotherapy to help me deal with the grief.

She was right, of course. I had no idea what I was in for, but she knew. Caring for my guy was like a full-time job, with several trips to the doctor each week, hours-long transfusions, and a slew of medications to keep track of and dispense. There was some intense training required for maintaining his PICC line, the catheter portal for I.V. infusions, because Mike virtually had no immune system and any misstep could lead to a deadly infection. There was daily TPN to administer, the liquid nutrition that was delivered through the port to help stabilize his weight after a dramatic forty-pound loss. One day I lost it, finding myself in a heap on the kitchen floor, sobbing and totally melting down under the stress.

Although I did not have the luxury to get grief counseling during Mike's final months, I did eventually seek out the help I so desperately needed a few months after his passing. The grief counselors who attended to me at the hospital when my son died had referred me to a grief therapist, so I finally set up an appointment.

After hearing my story, the therapist told me that she was not equipped to handle a situation as intense as mine, to my utter amazement. I didn't realize therapists have a cap on the level of grief intensity they can manage in a patient! So, I left her office feeling pretty disheartened.

Fortunately, someone referred me to a therapist who specialized in grief counseling for deaths caused by addiction. I was so relieved when she agreed to work with me, and on a sliding scale no less. She had helped many bereaved parents of young people who had lost their battle with addiction. I knew in this therapist I had found the right fit.

How important is finding the right fit? Well, when you are searching for a therapist to guide you through what is likely to be the very worst chapter of your life, you need to pay close attention to your gut feeling during that initial interview. You should feel somewhat comfortable with the therapist, even at that very first meeting. If you sense there is a personality clash between you, then it's best to cut your losses and keep looking. He or she should be a good listener and seem warm and caring. This is the person with whom you will be revealing your innermost emotions, memories, and struggles, so take your time in finding the right match.

Therapists have a big bag of tools they will draw on during the sessions. They may favor specific types of psychotherapy for grieving patients, including cognitive behavioral therapy, interpersonal therapy, exposure therapy for trauma, and other modalities. Sessions are conducted in a one-on-one setting; however, the therapist may recommend that you also consider participating in a grief support group. Grief groups can be a source of peer support, a place to share your personal story with others who will definitely relate.

The therapist's role is to guide you through the stages of grief as they emerge. While there may be some helpful guidance and even resource materials provided, a significant portion of the session will involve the therapist simply listening. Their office setting is a safe, confidential space where you should feel free to talk about your deceased child and express your emotions openly. In this way, the therapist honors your child by accepting your emotions and not attempting to direct or teach you. I know for me, as I sat there week after week squeezing a drenched tissue in my hand, how much I appreciated that comfortable and welcoming place to just wail and grieve the deaths of my loved ones.

Some mothers may get a bit stuck along their grief journey. As I have mentioned previously, there is nothing wrong with taking as much time as you need to wind through the stages. Many people are aware of Elisabeth Kübler-Ross's Five Stages of Grief. However, understand that these stages do not necessarily unfold in chronological order. In fact, you might think you have reached a new stage in the grieving process only to regress back to anger or shock again. This is perfectly normal and understandable after the traumatic loss of a child.

However, there is a condition called prolonged grief disorder (P.G.D.), also referred to as complicated grief, particularly affecting grieving parents. Symptoms of P.G.D. include the common symptoms of grief, but they are persistent, sometimes not subsiding even after a year. They include:

- Have trouble focusing on little other than your child's death
- Have difficulty accepting the death, even after an extended period
- Feel intense sorrow and ruminate over the loss of the child
- Feel bitter about the child's death
- Feel numb or detached
- Feel intense feelings of loss or emptiness
- Unable to recall or ponder the positive experiences with your child
- Have an intense and persistent longing for the child
- Either being intently focused on, or will avoid, reminders of the child
- Feel that life no longer has meaning or purpose
- May have thoughts of suicide

A skilled grief therapist will recognize the signs and symptoms of P.G.D. and provide specialized interventions. These might involve weekly homework assignments that are designed to help you process the loss through loss-focused exercises. As therapy progresses, restoration-focused exercises help you to move forward. Examples of the restoration-focused activities are such things as creating plans for achieving new, or abandoned, life goals and returning to hobbies or activities you once enjoyed.

For many mothers who mourn a child's death, there is residual trauma that must be processed and healed. The trauma might be related to the shocking events surrounding the child's death, or even debilitating feelings of guilt or self-blame regarding the death. Post-traumatic stress disorder (P.T.S.D.) is common in parents who have lost a child in a shocking or intensely traumatizing manner.

When P.T.S.D. is present, there are some targeted interventions that can help soften the impact of the related memories of the death. Prolonged exposure therapy can be used to help you work through the disturbing memories or emotions. This is done through a process of reimaging the trauma while the therapist talks you through it, and also by physically revisiting the activities or places that trigger trauma symptoms. Both of these activities are done over a period of two or three months, with the goal of reducing the impact of the traumatic memories so you can move forward and heal.

Another trauma-related therapy is called eye movement desensitization reprocessing (E.M.D.R.). This is a short-term therapy that involves the therapist using a stimulus, either an object or their finger, which the patient tracks with their eyes in a back-and-forth motion. During these bilateral eye movements, the therapist will ask you to recall the distressing or traumatic events related to your child's death. As the E.M.D.R. therapy sessions progress, it becomes easier to discuss the memories as they slowly lose their intensity. E.M.D.R. is not a traditional form of therapy but is found to be an effective adjunctive therapy for reducing the symptoms of P.T.S.D.

Since experiencing residual feelings of anxiety is perfectly normal after the loss, do yourself a favor and make a point to avoid, or at least limit, any exposure to stress triggers. You may find, as I did, that you are hypersensitive to stressors. Even seemingly small issues, minor conflicts and such, can trigger a tidal wave of stress and anxiety. Be aware of your particular sensitivities and do your best to minimize contact with the sources of stress. It also helps to learn some stress-reduction coping skills, like deep breathing techniques and mindfulness meditation. These relaxation methods take some practice to master, but they can be accessed anywhere and at any time, and cost nothing. Managing stress should be a central aspect of your self-care efforts.

It should not be at all surprising that grieving mothers often fall into depression. It is important to be aware of the symptoms of depression so you can see a doctor if the symptoms persist for more than two weeks. Symptoms of depression include:

- Persistent feelings of sadness, despair, or hopelessness
- Loss of interest in the activities once enjoyed
- Changes in eating habits, resulting in sudden weight gain or loss
- Changes in sleeping patterns, such as insomnia or over-sleeping
- Slowed or agitated movements
- Irrational feelings of guilt or shame
- Fatigue
- Difficulty concentrating or making decisions
- Recurrent thoughts of death or suicide

Depression is highly treatable using a combination of psychotherapy and antidepressant drug therapy. The medication is initially trialed for four to six weeks. If the antidepressant causes more adverse effects than benefits, the doctor will move on to trial another medication. It is very common to trial two or more antidepressants before finding one that helps reduce the depression symptoms with the least amount of side effects.

Personally, I opted not to go on antidepressants, although my doctors at the time really pushed the medications. For a few years, at my annual physicals, the doctor would offer me a prescription for the antidepressants. I always declined because I didn't want to medicate myself through the grief journey. Of course, had I been suicidal I would not have hesitated for one minute, but since I wasn't, I felt that suffering through the emotions associated with a devastating loss is part of the natural human experience. I may be a glutton for punishment, but I didn't want to mask these normal emotions. I realize that many people do access antidepressants after a loss, and I support the use of these medications, knowing that they can save lives.

While I am an advocate for mothers accessing grief therapy to help manage the intense emotions after losing a child, I also realize that therapy isn't for everyone. If you fall into that camp, hopefully you have a couple of close friends or family members to be there for you in the aftermath. They do not need any special training, just a deep sense of compassion for a mother in mourning. Having someone who cares about you and your deceased child there for you, to just sit with you and allow you to weep freely, may be all that is really needed.

CHAPTER 17

Roll with It

From childhood, parents and teachers have taught us the importance of setting goals in life. We learned from an early age to aim for various benchmarks, like getting a college degree, starting a promising career, or finding a suitable spouse, that would help us to attain "success." These teachings always resonated with me because I am hardwired to be driven and goal-oriented. I believed what I was taught, that when you work hard and pursue your passions, you'll achieve your goals and, ultimately, succeed in life.

While there is some truth to that formula, I know now, with the luxury of hindsight, that this simplistic view of how life is supposed to play out happens to be deeply flawed. It relies on a shaky premise, that our expectations for life will be fulfilled as planned. When life delivers unexpected and devastating punches, and vaporizes that vision we'd had for our life, it can be highly destabilizing. The vision of my future always included *three* children . . . but then life threw me a sucker punch.

Since losing my son, I have learned the hard way that some life events are so devastating that all prior assumptions we had about our future simply no longer hold water. No amount of planning and elbow grease can guarantee us that life will go according to plan. A loss such as this is extremely humbling; it levels you and brings you to your knees. I now have a crystal clear understanding of just how fragile life really is, and how vulnerable *I* am. Losing my son truly has left me deeply wounded and forever altered.

It has taken me a few years, but I am slowly learning how to roll with it, to accept that life can force us to change our expectations and assumptions on a dime. I no longer cling to a preconceived vision of how my life will unfold. Never in my wildest dreams would I have thought that someday I would lose my child. But that harsh reality is my truth. I will be a grieving mother for the rest of my earthly life.

So, like an Etch-a-Sketch, we swipe away the image of our former self and use those little knobs to scribble out a new one. This new version of self looks very different, for sure, and will require regular edits and adjustments as it takes shape. But approaching life after loss requires us to become more flexible, not only with our expectations for the future, but also for *ourselves*. For what we can realistically expect from ourselves. It is a new mindset that takes time to cultivate, but when you do come around it is actually quite freeing.

I am learning how to "let go and let God." I first heard this slogan at an Alcoholics Anonymous meeting that I attended with my son. Although it resonated with me back then, I admit that I still struggle with the concept. I have always operated under the delusion that I am in the driver's seat. Ha! Now, though, I do at least try to put my natural bull-headed determination aside, at least to some extent. In doing this, I make room for my new life, a life without my son, to emerge and unfold without forcing any predetermined outcomes. I am learning to roll with it, to be more flexible, to adjust and to *relent*. It has finally dawned on me that I need to stop trying to out-muscle God.

This doesn't mean we give up on our hopes and dreams! Our child would never, ever want us to do that. Rolling with it simply means to go easy on ourselves as we navigate this new landscape instead of climbing back onto the hamster wheel and starting to run again. By slowing down and allowing the ripples of sorrow to etch new facets into our beings, we can slowly come to accept this new pared down version of ourselves. Yes, we are missing a chunk of our heart and soul, but we can still function. We can still think and create. We still have years of life to live, purpose to fulfill, joy to experience, and people to love.

I admit that when the loss is fresh, it is impossible to imagine functioning at all, much less as a productive woman with purpose. That first year is so brutal and raw, as we gut out the holidays, our child's birthday, Mother's Day, and every other cultural reminder that your child is gone. So, for all the newly grief-stricken mothers reading this, just roll with it. Feel the pain. Gut it out. Don't put any expectations on yourself at all. Proceed at your pace along your sorrowful journey. As C.S. Lewis once wrote, "There is great good in bearing sorrow patiently" (cited in *A Severe Mercy* by Sheldon Vanauken, page 189).

In time—and it can take a *long* time—you'll begin to draw a new version of yourself on that Etch-a-Sketch. This version may have the sad eyes of a grieving mother, but it will also emanate the fresh new energy of renewed hope. Trust me on this . . . you will get stronger.

A mother's grief journey is unlike any other kind of grief. The road is riddled with twists and turns, bumps and dips. Put no effort into trying to control the ride. Instead, buckle up and just roll with it. Pretty soon, up there on the horizon, you'll see a road sign for an exit called Hope.

CHAPTER 18

Embrace Hope and Seek Joy

In the months, and sometimes even years, following a child's death, the very idea of ever feeling hopeful or joy-filled again seems pretty implausible. Those virtues were crushed right along with our spirit the day we said that final goodbye. Our child, regardless of their age at death, was our life, our blood, our very heart and soul. He or she was an integral part of our own life story, of who we were at the time they were born, and the person we became over the years we were blessed to have them. These young people bore witness to our lives, as we did theirs. Now that we are separated, the thought that we might ever feel joyful again seems farfetched.

When I look back at myself six or seven years ago, I can attest to the bleak existence I was living soon after Matthew died. As a people pleaser, I would feign joy when the situation called for it, but rarely, if ever, was it sincere. I honestly didn't have any modicum of hopefulness or joy left in me. I felt empty and devoid of any authentic happiness, but put on the false mask when it felt appropriate in a given situation. This charade was born of a valiant effort to avoid being the sad sack who brought everybody down at a family event or party, on those rare occasions that I even felt up to attending.

My precious grandchildren were about the only sources of pure joy that I was to experience in those early days after Matt and Mike's deaths. How can you not feel hope for these sweet babes' futures, or experience a genuine sense of joy just by being in their presence? But truly, that was about it. I was overwhelmingly hopeless and joyless for a very long time.

And then one day, it just happened. A long-lost remnant of my then deadened spirit began to percolate back to the surface. I have no idea what the catalyst was for this change of heart, but I am grateful that I seem to be hardwired to seek joy. I guess the Holy Spirit had decided I had wallowed long enough and it was time to locate some renewed hope for what was left of my life.

Believe me when I tell you that, one day, and totally out of the blue, you will wake up feeling just a little bit lighter. This is not a shift that you can plan for because it occurs at the most random time, uncorrelated to any particular event. In fact, there will be many things that take place after losing your son or daughter that *should* make you feel hopeful or bring you some joy, but will utterly fail in this regard. No, this subtle, almost imperceptible change in your attitude occurs for no logical reason, but is always a reflection of God's perfect timing.

I realize the title of this chapter proposes a tall order. How do you even begin to muster the energy to embrace hope again? To us, all hope was dashed when our child passed away. And hope for what, exactly? I admit that in the early months after my losses I hoped for something, all right. I hoped for a truck to veer off the road and just take me out when walking my dogs every day. Now, of course,

I am very grateful that I actually returned home safely after those dog walks. That's because I am blessed now to once again experience hope, and that feels really good. In fact, hope is the high-octane fuel that powers me through my days.

Okay, fine, but then what about joy? I mean, come on! How can a mother who has been completely broken by the death of her child ever again experience that elusive state-of-being referred to as "joyful?" True joy emanates from within, coursing through our veins and expressed outwardly with twinkly eyes and a big, toothy smile. You may be utterly convinced that feeling joyful is something you will never experience again . . . until you do.

Yes, out of nowhere something completely unexpected will trigger the sensation of joy. Suddenly, you may feel your heart leap or dance in your chest at the sight of something. At first, you might even try to suppress the feeling because it feels inappropriate to experience happiness and joy when your baby is no longer on the earth. Eventually, though, you will stop putting up a fight. You will give yourself permission to feel happy again.

The human spirit is pretty amazing in its ability to overcome adversity. Throughout our lives we will all suffer setbacks, disappointments, and loss. Loss comes in many different varieties: the loss of a loved one, a divorce or breakup, a job loss, or the loss of good health, just to name a few. By the time we hit middle age, we are fully aware that loss hurts, pure and simple, and that we can expect to feel sad for a period of time as we heal from the loss. But just as day follows night, we do eventually pull ourselves out of the funk and move forward. It is very hard to keep the human spirit tied up in bondage for too long because that goes against nature.

When it comes to the very worst loss imaginable, the one we have experienced, you should expect the rebounding process to take a while. Some of us might be more resilient than others and return to a hopeful, joyful demeanor sooner rather than later, but most grieving mothers expect their healing process to be lengthy. Even if you truly want to feel normal again, and you pine for the return of your former joyful nature, chances are it will be some time before that day arrives, when joy peeks out from behind the shadows to surprise you.

But, oh, when that day comes, embrace it! Seize the moment and recognize it for what it is—a sign that you are still a living, breathing woman with a heart that continues to beat. Thus, the stage is set to once again experience happiness.

Seek joy in the things you might have buried while in deep grief, like your passion for art or music, for photography, travel, writing, or theater. Seek joy in nature, in the sparkling ocean, colorful sunsets, and twinkling stars. Seek joy in your spouse, your children or grandkids, your best friends, and your pets. But mostly, seek joy in your faith—that it has survived and remains the glue that holds your broken parts together. Dig deeper into your faith beliefs. Rekindle your thirst for truth in the Scriptures, and nurture a more sincere and prayerful relationship with Him.

The return of hope and joy to your life may feel a bit foreign to you at first, but don't turn your back on these promising signs of life. Instead, just embrace them and be glad.

> May the God of hope fill you with all joy and peace in believing, so that you may abound in hope by the power of the Holy Spirit.
>
> —Romans 15:13 NAB

CHAPTER 19

Rising from the Ruins

When we grieving mommas eventually do rise from the ruins, it certainly won't be a Superman moment, victoriously exploding skyward with fist held high. It is anything but. After simmering in the ash pit of sorrow for so long, we are lucky to crawl out of the ruins of what used to be our life, tripping and stumbling as we go.

Everything about this new life is so *hard*. We feel physically weaker than we once were. We feel hollowed out, numb, and beaten down. We are exhausted from walking around with P.T.S.D. and painful memories swarming through our heads all day. We are jumpy and on edge, quick to snap at the slightest provocation. We are emotionally fragile, on the edge of tears much of the time, feeling literally starved in the absence of hearing our child's name.

We envy our friends who have never been touched by such a tragedy. What is that like? We wonder in amazement. What does it feel like to have everyone present at the Thanksgiving table or at the family Christmas party? What does it feel like to be able to easily answer someone's inquiry, "So, how many kids do you have?" without tripping over a pre-packaged response to that monster trigger? I can't even imagine that kind of life anymore.

When we finally rise from the ruins, we will do so by taking baby steps, gingerly peeking out of the dark hole searching for a supportive hand to grab. It is scary when we first enter real life again. But someday, we will just know that the time has come to gather our courage and try to function as a "normal" person again.

So, what will it be like "out there?" What will it feel like to attend social events, work functions, and family gatherings again? How do we even make small talk? For me, that is one of the biggest challenges of beginning the process of living life again—that mindless, insipid small talk. How do you return to engaging in vacuous conversations again after going through something so life altering and huge? It feels hardly worth the effort, to be honest. I can remember how, early on, I tried to make conversation at a small gathering and really struggled to even contribute. Part of me wanted to shout, "How can you be talking about something so meaningless? My son died!" but thankfully, I managed to restrain myself.

As time moves on, little by little you will begin to adjust to your new normal. You will feel a bit lopsided, with one limb now missing from your body, and you never quite feel stable on your feet, but those feet still move you forward, one step at a time. There is a slow gathering of momentum, a kind of spiritual momentum, like an invisible force that gently pushes you to take the next step, and the next.

In 2015, when I was emerging from the ruins almost two years after my son's death, I decided it was time to get back in shape. This was a very big step for me because the act of joining a new gym sent a life-affirming signal to myself that I actually did care about my health and I wanted to stay alive after all.

As I mentioned in an earlier chapter, I joined a boot camp. It featured buff twenty-somethings leading intense workouts in a warehouse without air conditioning. For sure I was at least a decade older than most of the members, but that did not deter me. I was determined to get in shape.

One day, while running laps outside in the hot sun before the class began, I swear I sensed my son in my midst, clear as day, prodding me to keep going, to not give up. I literally conjured up a mental image of him coaching me, "You can do it, Mom, don't give up! Keep going." For the rest of the workout, I imagined him watching me, so I made an extra effort to please my son—to make him proud of me while I proceeded to sweat the sorrow right out of my pores.

Rising from the ruins is scary, but in an odd way it's also a little exhilarating. It almost feels like you've been given a chance at a whole new life, an unexpected gift after losing your child that grim day. But not every mom in her depths of grief will be willing to grab that outreached hand and pull themselves out of the pit of despair.

Each mother is a unique individual with her own emotional wiring. Some mothers will rebound sooner than others. In the end, most grieving mothers will ultimately emerge from the ruins, each in her own time. But some are so crushed by the loss that they remain hunkered down in their sorrow. Sadly, these mothers are comfortable there, having decided to take up a permanent residence in the shadows rather than choosing to rejoin the living.

I think it's a shame to give up on life altogether. Yes, our lives will never be the same without our precious child. But surely there are other people in each of our lives who are worth making the effort for. This is especially the case when the mother has other children. She may have tragically lost a child, but why choose to live as if the other children are gone, too? My hope is that the grieving mothers who are stuck in the ash pile eventually receive the help and support they so deserve. They, too, still have a life to live.

For the women who have simmered in a stew of sadness long enough, and are finally open to taking a shot at life again, this moment becomes the turning point toward renewal. Up until this pivotal moment, those early months of grief held you captive. They owned you. During that dark chapter, you did what you could just to survive each day. And then, slowly, you began making choices that benefited your mental and spiritual wellbeing. Maybe you saw a therapist, maybe you went back to church, maybe you kept a gratitude journal, or maybe you started taking daily walks. Over the months and years, you grew stronger. One day, hope said hello to you again, and this time you responded to the salutation.

Now you are standing up, straight and tall, having successfully dug your way out of the ruins. You might then turn your face skyward and ask, even *plead*, "Tell me, God, what should I do with my life now?"

No matter how hard you strain to hear the answer, chances are you won't receive an audible response from heaven. It just doesn't work that way. God works within us, in the depths of our hearts. He works through the people who populate our lives. He inspires action from us in the most unusual ways at the most unexpected times. Just remain open, trusting, and alert. You made it out of the ash heap. You are standing upright. Now, allow God to reveal His plan for your life.

CHAPTER 20
Honor Your Child

In my opinion, there is no greater honor bestowed upon a woman than the gift of raising a child. Since I became a mother with my firstborn, Sarah, back in 1986, I have been perpetually in awe of the astonishing power of motherhood. I honestly had no idea, prior to beginning my journey as a mother, that having children would bless me so profoundly. Nothing in my first thirty years of life even came close to the pure happiness I have experienced as a mother. Oh yes, it is hard. It is scary and exhausting and infuriating—and sometimes all of these emotions occur within a moment's time. But for me, nothing fills me to overflowing like being someone's mother.

When the unthinkable happens and a child is taken from us, an enormous void is left, a constant reminder of what we have lost. As a woman, you feel gutted, like your insides have literally been surgically removed. This human being, a person you had raised, who walked on the planet and impacted other people's lives, is suddenly gone. Now, in their absence, how on earth do you give back anything remotely close to the love and joy they gave you during their short time here? Our lovely, amazing children should be honored, and guess what? Honor him or her you shall do.

When I sat down to begin writing this final chapter, I found myself overcome, tears rolling down my face. Just the idea of honoring our lost children is wrapped up in layers of love and loss so thick with emotion that it hurts to even contemplate the gesture. The dictionary's definition of the verb, "honor", doesn't come close to what I am trying to convey here. Merriam-Webster states the meaning of "honor" this way: "To regard or treat someone with admiration and respect; to regard or treat with honor," and "To give special recognition to; to confer honor on." Okay, well I guess in a general sense that definition works, but only in the most superficial way. When I think about honoring my child, a person who blessed and enriched my life so abundantly, I want to do all that—but times one hundred . . . a thousand even. I'd bet all us moms feel that way. It is difficult to wrap our arms around the hugeness of honoring our child. But how can we *not* honor them in some way, whether large or small?

For me personally, honoring Matthew's memory means never forgetting the innumerable ways he touched my life, his daughter's life, and every single family member, friend, or colleague's life who was blessed to know him. I want to keep his memory alive, to hear his name still spoken. I cling to my memories of Matthew because they bring me immense comfort and joy, even contrasted against the sorrowful reality that he is no longer here. Thoughts of him still fill me with a kind of soothing warmth, yet another sign that love is a living energy that is not extinguished when the breathing process stops.

All of us who have had to say goodbye to a child are driven by a deep subconscious desire to honor them in some way. We may not be aware of where our ideas to memorialize them even come from. It has been truly beautiful to witness the diverse ways my fellow grieving mothers have honored, and continue to honor, their deceased children. While we obviously realize we cannot bring our son or daughter back, and that we must move forward in our lives, we enjoy making special gestures that keep them alive in hearts and minds.

Until I sat down to write this final chapter, I hadn't really thought about the variety of ways I have honored Matt's memory since his death. But in allowing myself to look back, I was pretty surprised. They were just small gestures, little things I did to keep his memory alive. Like when his daughter, Grace, was four, I bought her a Ninja Turtle swimsuit because her daddy was obsessed with Ninja Turtles. When she was eight, I introduced her, along with my grandson, to Creepy Crawlers, one of Matt's favorite toys in childhood, by snagging a 1980s machine off eBay. We made a bunch of colorful rubber bugs to commemorate his birthday, along with a birthday cake festooned with bright blue frosting in honor of his nickname, Boy Blue. My daughters and I still cook up his favorite tuna casserole recipe, and mention him regularly in our conversations. I dress up his gravesite on several occasions throughout the year, stopping at the local Dollar Store on the way to grab bargain balloons and decorations, and his favorite candy bar.

His peers have honored Matt's memory, too, by visiting his resting place, honoring him at their weddings, or mentioning him on social media. Just five months after his passing, his former high school baseball coach organized a tribute alumni game in Matthew's memory. Prior to the event, one of his teammates had spearheaded the effort to have an eight-foot banner made, designed with Matt's name, class, and jersey number, and had it installed on the outfield fence of the ball field, and covered. Right before the alumni game was to begin, with thirty-eight baseball players on the field, stands full of loved ones, and reporters from two newspapers present, the banner was unveiled. My heart just melted. The coach then led a moment of silence before asking me to toss the first (very wild) pitch.

Together we honored my beautiful son on the baseball field where he had experienced so much joy during his teens.

And then there are the events. One year I participated in an Out of the Darkness walk for suicide awareness, our team enthusiastically raising the most money for the fundraiser that day. We walked for miles wearing t-shirts emblazoned with Matt's photo. Then, one year I joined about a hundred people at the beach to decorate lanterns with the names of our lost loved ones. At dusk, we lit the lanterns, carving a gorgeous colorful trail across the sand. Another year my daughters and I participated in a Night of Remembrance event to honor children lost to addiction. One by one, family members who'd lost a child took the stage, holding large framed photos of the child and sharing with the audience about how very special they were.

There are so many ways to honor your child, including making donations to causes or fundraisers that are close to your heart. For me that has been the American Foundation for Suicide Prevention, the National Alliance on Mental Illness, and the Salvation Army. In this small way, I have hoped to help others in need of resources and support for battling mental health disorders or addiction.

Somehow, with God's grace, I was able to complete the manuscript for my memoir by Matt's fifth memorial date. That day, when I visited his grave, I placed the manuscript on the headstone and, looking up at the sky said, "I did it, Blue! I wrote your story." After that, I drove to a nearby theater that was playing *Beautiful Boy*, the movie version of a book by David Sheff that had helped me immensely during his disease. I sat there alone in the dark with tears streaming down my face. The movie had just been released, so it was a fitting way to honor my son on his fifth memorial date.

I have witnessed countless ways that other mothers have chosen to honor their child over the years; many of these women are featured in this book. One mother created a memorial rock garden in a town square, with lovingly painted rocks, each bearing the name of a deceased child and beautifully arranged in a tranquil setting in which mothers can rest and reflect. One mom organized several neighborhood drug awareness campaigns, with city officials and hundreds of participants in attendance to witness the grieving parents holding posters featuring photos of their child lost to opioids. Some mothers who lost their child to a fatal disease have honored their memories by participating in cancer walks, blood drives, organ donor programs, and creating foundations in their child's memory. Some mothers honor their child through creative channels, allowing their child's spirit to inspire amazing art, or to create beautiful graphics that help express the grief journey. One mother organized a weekly support group in her son's honor, a safe place where parents can convene and support each other. One mom made a public service announcement for a major health provider about the importance of bike helmet safety after losing her son to a traumatic brain injury. One mother established a college scholarship in memory of her child. All the mothers provide support and compassion for other parents who are reeling from the loss of a child. The list of ways to honor a child is literally endless.

I cite these examples for good reason. I want to shine a light on what a grieving mother is capable of accomplishing, even after suffering such a devastating blow. Even though mired in immense emotional pain, there is a desire—a *need*—to do something special in that child's memory. Again, these gestures can be as simple as wearing your child's favorite color, cooking his or her favorite dish, or listening to their favorite music on their birthday. Any gesture, no matter how small, that is done in honor of the deceased child can help keep their memory alive.

Many of us have discovered a special connection to something in nature that reminds us of our child. For me, it is yellow butterflies.

Whenever I see a yellow butterfly, I just know it is my son saying hello, letting me know he is still here with me in some form. One of the mothers featured in this book fancies bees as the symbol of her son's presence; for another mother it is hummingbirds that represent her son, while yet another mom cites ducks! While this may sound silly to some, to us these little creatures have taken on a special significance in our grief journey. When we spot them flitting about in the world, they make us *smile*, not cry. To us, these creatures symbolize our child's spirit and actually help keep our son or daughter near to our hearts. You see . . . even nature honors our child.

For someone in the raw early stages of grief, know that the inspiration to honor your son or daughter will emerge when you least expect it. Suddenly, an idea will pop into your head, something that just came to you out of nowhere. It might be as simple as planting a tree in their honor or creating a beautiful scrapbook of their life. No matter what springs to mind, know that it is only the beginning of many more ideas to come. These brainstorms will continue to bubble up to the surface along your grief journey, evolving and growing as time passes. Whether it is simply recalling a funny memory of your child that starts a conversation about them, or an amazing undertaking done in your child's name, you will each find your own special ways to honor your beloved child . . . because that purest of love, the love between a mother and her child, will inspire you.

The End

Final Thoughts

When I embarked on this project in January, it was easy to predict that the chapters I'd receive from the contributing mothers would be powerful. I knew the basic stories of most of the moms, having met them and interacted with them over these past seven years since joining the "club." However, I had no idea how rich and layered and truly remarkable each and every story would be.

As I sat at my computer reading each incoming story, I found myself journeying with them through their pain. While I read along, I felt a sisterhood with these inspiring ladies. Often I would nod and say aloud, "Me, too!" as I read their experiences with tears running down my face. Anyone who has experienced the loss of a child feels such deep empathy and connection with other parents who have gone through the same tragedy.

Over the months of interacting with these mothers, checking in periodically, cheering them on, and offering my support in any way I could along the way, I sometimes felt like a counselor. I knew in advance how painful it would be for them to relive the dark days and write their stories, having already gone through the process myself. And yes, as predicted, each and every contributing mom experienced gut-wrenching pain while writing her chapter. Some even had to take a week or two off to recover before returning to the project. Still, these strong women forged ahead and never gave up.

As I stated early on, the purpose of writing this book was to give newly grieving mothers a sense of hope amid their hopelessness. I can personally attest to the excruciating emotions a woman must work through when coming to grips with such an unfathomable loss. Hope is the very last thing you think you will ever experience again.

But, alas! God, the master Potter, does work His wonders. He gathers nuggets from the bits and pieces of what is left of us, cobbling together a new, slightly altered, version of us in that lump of clay. In our brokenness, He guides us toward new purpose, setting us on a course toward renewed hope.

In their stories, the women all described the exact same pattern of loss, grief, and the emerging spark of hope that defies all expectations. Mostly, these women are living examples of resilience and strength. We are not just a sad club of grieving mothers—we are *survivors*. Tough as boot leather on some days, and meek as lambs on others. Admittedly, our moods shift all over the place, sometimes locking into a really positive space, and other times, not so much. But we are human with hearts still beating, hoping to make a difference in another woman's life; to assure her that, indeed, hope does spring from a mother's broken heart. You just watch.

About the Author

THERESA ANTHONY is the author of the memoir, *My 13th Station: A Mother Shares Her Son's Tragic Battle with Depression, Alcoholism, and Demons.* This current book, *Hope Springs from a Mother's Broken Heart: 11 Mothers Share How They Survived the Loss of a Child*, represents the natural evolution of her grief journey, and a wonderful opportunity to help other grieving mothers. As a freelance writer of over two decades, Ms. Anthony now devotes much of her time to writing within the mental health and addiction recovery space. In this capacity, she hopes to make a meaningful contribution toward nudging individuals into treatment through her compassionate, informative content. Ms. Anthony continues to find joy in her family and friends, her four beautiful grandchildren, creating artwork and jewelry for her Etsy shop, and her Catholic faith.

Visit Theresa: www.TheresaAnthony.com
Facebook: www.facebook.com/theresaanthonyauthor
Instagram: @theresaanthonyauthor
Twitter: @TheresaA_author

Please kindly leave a book review on Amazon,
or on any of my social media platforms!